D1219902

CLASSICS IN EDUCATION

Lawrence A. Cremin, General Editor

☆ ☆ ☆

THE REPUBLIC AND THE SCHOOL
Horace Mann on the Education of Free Men
Edited by Lawrence A. Cremin

AMERICAN IDEAS ABOUT ADULT EDUCATION
1710–1951
Edited by C. Hartley Grattan

DEWEY ON EDUCATION
Introduction and Notes by Martin S. Dworkin

THE SUPREME COURT AND EDUCATION
Edited by David Fellman

INTERNATIONAL EDUCATION
A Documentary History
Edited by David G. Scanlon

CRUSADE AGAINST IGNORANCE
Thomas Jefferson on Education
Edited by Gordon C. Lee

CHINESE EDUCATION UNDER COMMUNISM
Edited by Chang-tu Hu

CHARLES W. ELIOT AND POPULAR EDUCATION
Edited by Edward A. Krug

WILLIAM T. HARRIS ON EDUCATION
(in preparation)
Edited by Martin S. Dworkin

THE *EMILE* OF JEAN JACQUES ROUSSEAU
Selections
Translated and Edited by William Boyd

THE MINOR EDUCATIONAL WRITINGS OF
JEAN JACQUES ROUSSEAU
Selected and Translated by William Boyd

PSYCHOLOGY AND THE SCIENCE OF EDUCATION
Selected Writings of Edward L. Thorndike
Edited by Geraldine M. Joncich

THE NEW-ENGLAND PRIMER
Introduction by Paul Leicester Ford

BENJAMIN FRANKLIN ON EDUCATION
Edited by John Hardin Best

THE COLLEGES AND THE PUBLIC
1787–1862
Edited by Theodore Rawson Crane

TRADITIONS OF AFRICAN EDUCATION
Edited by David G. Scanlon

NOAH WEBSTER'S AMERICAN SPELLING BOOK
Introductory Essay by Henry Steele Commager

VITTORINO DA FELTRE
AND OTHER HUMANIST EDUCATORS
By William Harrison Woodward
Foreword by Eugene F. Rice, Jr.

DESIDERIUS ERASMUS
CONCERNING THE AIM AND METHOD
OF EDUCATION
By William Harrison Woodward
Foreword by Craig R. Thompson

JOHN LOCKE ON EDUCATION
Edited by Peter Gay

CATHOLIC EDUCATION IN AMERICA
A Documentary History
Edited by Neil G. McCluskey, S.J.

THE AGE OF THE ACADEMIES
Edited by Theodore R. Sizer

HEALTH, GROWTH, AND HEREDITY
G. Stanley Hall on Natural Education
Edited by Charles E. Strickland and Charles Burgess

TEACHER EDUCATION IN AMERICA
A Documentary History
Edited by Merle L. Borrowman

THE EDUCATED WOMAN IN AMERICA
Selected Writings of Catharine Beecher,
Margaret Fuller, and M. Carey Thomas
Edited by Barbara M. Cross

EMERSON ON EDUCATION
Selections
Edited by Howard Mumford Jones

ECONOMIC INFLUENCES UPON EDUCATIONAL PROGRESS IN THE UNITED STATES, 1820–1850
By Frank Tracy Carlton
Foreword by Lawrence A. Cremin

QUINTILIAN ON EDUCATION
Selected and Translated by William M. Smail

ROMAN EDUCATION FROM CICERO TO QUINTILIAN
By Aubrey Gwynn, S.J.

Quintilian on Education

Selected and Translated, with an Introduction, by

WILLIAM M. SMAIL

TEACHERS COLLEGE PRESS
TEACHERS COLLEGE, COLUMBIA UNIVERSITY
NEW YORK

Library of Congress Catalog Card
Number 66–13554

Originally published
by Oxford University Press in 1938
Reprinted by permission
of Oxford University Press

Manufactured in the United States of America
by the William Byrd Press, Inc.
Richmond, Virginia

Preface

"Grave Quintilian," propounder of the "justest rules and clearest method joined"—so goes the well-known verdict by the most Augustan of English poets about the most Roman of colonials. Alexander Pope's esteem is not surprising, for Quintilian fairly exudes the Newtonian virtues of order and reasonableness. Even his criticism of his archrival, Seneca the Younger, was couched in polite and balanced phrases.

The *Institutes* is not, as Professor Smail implies, a textbook for boys, but rather an encyclopedia for adults. Men of letters in the eighteenth century could turn to it for literary judgments; educators, for guidelines on curriculum development and pedagogy. No other classical treatise served this dual purpose.

However, one must guard against an exaggerated view of Quintilian's influence. The twelve books of the *Institutes* were forbidding to all but the industrious, and their detail effectively kept them out of young hands. The longer educational shadow, it may be argued, was cast by Quintilian's chief mentor, Cicero. Like Lord Chesterfield, many claimed that if Quintilian was the best book "to form an orator," Cicero's *De oratore* was the best "to finish one." Here was found the ideal of the perfect orator, who united philosophy with eloquence.

It was an ideal that Quintilian imperfectly canonized. He accorded civil law a cavalier treatment that would have embarrassed the author of the *Ad Herennium;* his praise of music, geometry, and astronomy was qualified by his excluding them from the rhetor's program. Natural philosophy was almost absorbed into moral philosophy, and this was left precariously poised on commonplace maxims as a result of his suspicion of the philosophical schools.

The austerity of Quintilian's program for the intellectual training of the orator meant that the full potential of Cicero's lofty ideal could not be realized. For Quintilian, eloquence, interpreted narrowly as rhetoric, prevailed over philosophy. Perhaps it could not have been otherwise. The bar of the Principate was undoubtedly less congenial to the Ciceronian version of the universal man than was the Republican forum. But one cannot help wondering if, indeed, Quintilian exhausted all the possibilities, whether in trying to be politically respectable he did not sacrifice too much content to method.

The best general introduction to classical education may be found in H. I. Marrou, *A History of Education in Antiquity* (New York, 1956). D. L. Clark, *Rhetoric in Greco-Roman Education* (New York, 1957) is sympathetic to rhetoric; M. L. Clarke, *Rhetoric at Rome* (London, 1953), moderately critical. The legal context is presented by E. P. Parks in *The Roman Rhetorical Schools as a Preparation for the Courts under the Early Empire* (Baltimore, 1945). For a revisionist viewpoint, see G. Kennedy, "An Estimate of Quintilian," *American Journal of Philology,* LXXXII (1962), 130–146.

JAMES S. HOCKLEY

Teachers College
Columbia University

QUINTILIAN ON EDUCATION

BEING
A TRANSLATION OF SELECTED
PASSAGES FROM THE
INSTITUTIO ORATORIA
WITH AN
INTRODUCTORY ESSAY ON
QUINTILIAN, HIS ENVIRONMENT
AND HIS
THEORY OF EDUCATION

BY
WILLIAM M. SMAIL, M.A.
RECTOR OF PERTH ACADEMY

OXFORD
AT THE CLARENDON PRESS
1938

CONTENTS

Book II

Book XII

INTRODUCTION

1. *Biographical*

Marcus Fabius Quintilianus was one of that distinguished band of writers who during the first century A.D. made Spain famous as a centre of Roman culture and of creative activity in literature. The list of these Spanish writers of Latin masterpieces is a long one, including the two Senecas, father and son, the poets Lucan and Martial, the prose writers Pomponius Mela, Columella, and Quintilian. We should err, however, if we imagined these men as consciously stressing the fact of their Spanish birth. They thought and wrote as citizens of the Roman Empire which for military and administrative purposes recognized provincial boundaries but which bound the varied elements together by the gifts of a common language and a common law. Filelfo in the fifteenth century professed to detect in Quintilian a certain 'Spanish barbarism', but it would seem to be as hard to discover as the so-called 'Patavinity' of the Roman historian Livy. Mommsen tells us that Roman civilization gained ground in Spain more rapidly than in any other province especially in regard to literature, and the range of interest as well as the high level of literary merit shown in the work of the Spanish writers above-mentioned amply confirms his statement and offers an interesting proof of the success of Roman methods in the civilizing of southern Europe and of the receptivity of the provincials themselves.

Quintilian was born about A.D. 35 in the little town of Calagurris on the upper waters of the Ebro. His father was probably a teacher of rhetoric. It is doubtful whether the young Quintilian acquired his early education in Spain or at Rome; inscriptions suggest that the resources of the province in this direction were already ample. It is, however, certain that he was in Rome in early manhood 'devilling' for the famous pleader Domitius Afer at some time between A.D. 50 and 58, with opportunities of hearing and meeting Seneca at the height of his power and influence. Domitius died in A.D. 58 or 59 and Quintilian apparently returned to Spain to practise as a declaimer and teacher of rhetoric there.

We next hear of him as brought back to Rome by Galba in the year A.D. 68, and it can only have been a few years later, early in the reign of Vespasian, that he received the official appointment as Professor of Rhetoric at Rome which Jerome's Chronicle wrongly assigns to the year A.D. 88. The institution of Professorships of Greek and Latin Rhetoric by the Emperor Vespasian, duly recorded by Suetonius, was an innovation of great importance in the history of Roman education, marking as it does the first official recognition of the state's responsibility in the matter of public instruction.

The stipend attached to Quintilian's chair was equivalent to nearly £900 per annum, and this was supplemented by the gifts of grateful clients and pupils. For some twenty years, from A.D. 70 to 90, he held this position as a civil servant under three emperors, Vespasian, Titus, and Domitian, recognized by his contemporaries as the foremost teacher of rhetoric in Rome. Thus the poet Martial, writing in the year A.D. 84 addresses him in the well-known lines:

Quintiliane, vagae moderator summe iuventae,
Gloria Romanae, Quintiliane, togae.

As this tribute implies, Quintilian was a pleader as well as a teacher. Perhaps his most famous case was his defence of the Jewish Queen Berenice in a suit in which the Queen herself acted as judge. This is referred to in the *Institutio* (iv. 1. 19), and there are a sufficient number of other references to his conduct of actual cases to assure us that the theoretical instruction of the class-room was in constant touch with the practice of the courts and that his activities as teacher and pleader were closely co-ordinated. Thus when he came to write his book on the training of the orator he was able to draw from rich stores of practical knowledge and experience.

Quintilian retired from his official position as Professor of Rhetoric about the year A.D. 90 and was soon engaged in the writing of his great work the *Institutio Oratoria*. He was now made tutor to the grand-nephews and heirs of the Emperor Domitian, the two sons of Flavius Clemens; through the influence of Clemens he received the consular insignia, or more accurately the privileges of consular name and rank.

A career of such conspicuous success made Quintilian a notable exception to the rule so emphatically stated by Juvenal in his seventh Satire, that teachers of rhetoric were despised and underpaid. The satirist notes the exception and explains that Quintilian is one of the lucky ones, rarer than white crows, to whom Fortune is uniformly kind:

si Fortuna volet, fies de rhetore consul;
si volet haec eadem, fies de consule rhetor.

His happiness, however, was clouded about the time of his retiral by the loss of his young wife (aged 19) and of his two sons to whose education he had dedicated at least in part the labour involved in the writing of the *Institutio*. In the preface to Book VI he speaks in touching terms of the successive losses he had sustained and of the disappointment of the high hopes he had formed for his little Quintilian.

In addition to the massive *Institutio*, the composition of which occupied little more than two years, Quintilian wrote a tract on 'the Causes of the Corruption of Eloquence' and probably published some of his more notable Declamations. The date of his death is unknown.

Such, in brief outline, are the facts known about the life of our author, Spaniard, orator and teacher, civil servant and tutor to the Imperial family. His great work, the *Institutio Oratoria* in twelve books, was designed as a text-book for the instruction of the son of Marcellus Victorius and the author's own sons, who died before the book was finished. It embodies the results of Quintilian's experience as a teacher of rhetoric at Rome over a period of twenty years, and sums up all that was valuable in the countless hand-books of rhetoric which had appeared in the century which divides Quintilian from Cicero. The outstanding qualities of the work are practical sagacity and good sense. At every point theory is checked by practical experience either in the school or in the law-courts, and the dry bones of rhetorical dogma are clothed in the living flesh of a great teacher's human interests. To the modern reader the title 'The Training of the Orator' is not attractive; we are inclined to be suspicious of rhetoric and oratory, and few of us associate higher education with proficiency in public speaking. 'Mere rhetoric' is the comment with which we dismiss those flights of eloquence which we instinctively distrust. Yet, if we are to understand the Roman view of education in its developed form, we must from the beginning keep it clearly in view that for the Romans rhetoric was the main element in higher education, and that they counted only that man properly educated who by his gifts of oratory could duly serve his country. That of course is not the whole account of the matter; we shall see in our author's own account the foundations upon which this practical citizenship rests. But before attempting to discuss the content of Quintilian's book, let us consider briefly the way in which educational theory and practice had developed at Rome before his time.

2. *Roman Theory of Education before Quintilian's Time*

Throughout the Republican period and for the first hundred years of the Empire the education of his children was a matter left entirely in the hands of the Roman paterfamilias. Even Augustus had no conception of organized public instruction as an instrument in his campaign for the betterment of Roman morals. Education, being thus a matter of private interest, tended to lag far behind the standards of Greece. Cicero in the *De Republica* (iv. 3) tells us that this is the only point on which Polybius indicts the negligence of Roman institutions. 'Our countrymen', Cicero continues, 'have thought that education ought not to be fixed or regulated by laws or given publicly and uniformly to all classes of society'.

During the period which preceded the Great Wars hardly any conscious theory of education existed in Roman minds beyond the common-sense view that boys and girls should be prepared for the responsibilities of life by association with and imitation of their elders.

This would mean in practice that the boy must learn by observation the details of house and farm management, that he must become skilled in the use of warlike weapons and in military drill, that he must acquire a sound knowledge of law and precedent, and above all of religious ritual. The girl too must be trained in domestic routine and in the countless practical duties falling to a woman's lot in a community which was primarily agricultural. The more formal discipline of this early period is to be found in the learning by heart of the Twelve Tables of the law and in the practice of those laborious methods of computation which the Roman duodecimal system of arithmetic involved.

A lively picture of the methods obtaining during this period is to be found in Plutarch's *Life of Cato the Censor* (North's translation, vol. iv, pp. 94–95):

'When his son was come to age of discretion and that he was able to learn anything, Cato himself did teach him, notwithstanding he had a slave in his house called Chilo (a very honest man and a good grammarian) who did also teach many another: but, as he himself said, he did not like a slave should rebuke his son nor pull him by the ears when peradventure he was not apt to take very suddenly that was taught him: neither would he have his son bound to a slave for so great a matter as that, as to have his learning of him. Wherefore he himself taught him his grammar, the law, and to exercise his body, not only to throw a dart, to play at the sword, to vault, to ride a horse and to handle all sorts of weapons, but also to fight with fists, to abide cold and heat, and to swim over a swift-running river. He said moreover that he wrote goodly histories in great letters with his own hand because his son might learn in his father's house the vertues of good men in times past, that he taking example by their doings should frame his life to excel them. He said also that he took as great heed of speaking any foul or unseemly words before his son, as he would have done if he had been before the Vestal Nuns.'

The dominant note of this early training is conservatism; *mos maiorum*, the way of our fathers, is the supreme guide in action, to depart from which is *superstitio*, a stepping beyond the rules of right conduct; and the result was the production of a type which is the glory of earlier Roman history, frugal, honest, brave and strong, but also unimaginative, unintellectual, hostile to innovation and experiment.

After the Great Wars, when 'captive Greece took captive her fierce conqueror and introduced the arts into rustic Latium', a new era in Roman education began. Made conscious of their intellectual shortcomings by contact with Greece, the Romans set themselves with their usual thoroughness to the task of acquiring culture. We may instance Aemilius Paullus and the Scipionic circle as typical of the new and wider interests. Their teachers were, for the most part, Greek, and the text-books available for literary study were Homer and the Greek tragic poets; thus the new Roman culture was based on the study of a foreign language and a foreign literature. Cato, the bitterest opponent of the new learning, lived to study in his eightieth year the works of Demosthenes and Thucydides.

Along with the study of language and literature came an awakening of interest in philosophy and rhetoric, subjects which had always held an important place in Greek higher education. Men of the old school, like Cato, dreaded and disliked the sophistry of which Carneades gave them a famous example on the occasion of the embassy of 155 B.C. After hearing Carneades plead first on the one side and then on the other with equal brilliance, Cato urged the dismissal of the three philosophers who formed the embassy from Athens and their expulsion from Rome lest they 'should infect and inchant the minds and affections of the youth and at unawares bring in an alteration of the manners and customs of the state,' (Bacon, *Advancement of Learning*, i). Already in 161 B.C. an edict of the senate had banished philosophers and Latin teachers of rhetoric from Rome, and in 92 B.C. the censors, of whom the eloquent and accomplished Lucius Licinius Crassus was one, suppressed the schools of Latin rhetoric as being 'schools of impudence' alien to the traditions of the state. But, in spite of the protests of conservatism, Greek rhetoric and Greek philosophy took their place quite definitely in higher education at Rome from the middle of the second century B.C. onwards.

The influence of these studies is manifest in every part of the work of Cicero. He was thoroughly at home among the masterpieces of Greece, as much so as in his own tongue and in his own land, and in his book *De Oratore* we have a polished presentation of the case for the new culture and the new education, a case which he amplified in the *Brutus* and the *Orator* ten years later. The orator in whom natural gifts have been developed and enriched by a liberal training in all branches of knowledge now takes his place as the ideal product of Roman education. In urging the claims of 'eloquence' it was no narrow sophistic conception which Cicero advanced; he meant an eloquence which embraced all accessible culture, both Greek and Latin, an eloquence which was a philosophy of life as well as a form of technical skill.

Thus in the *Tusculan Disputations* (i. 4) Cicero declares: 'I have always thought that to be able to speak copiously and elegantly on the most important subjects is the most perfect philosophy.' Again in the *Orator* (iv. 14) it is laid down as axiomatic that without philosophy we cannot fashion the eloquent man whom we are seeking. But philosophy is not enough; the task of the orator is a practical one, and he will be the true *vir eloquens* who, in the forum and in civil cases, will speak in such a way as to carry conviction, give delight, and change men's opinions. For himself Cicero confesses that he learned his oratory 'not in the workshops of the rhetors, but in the spacious walks of the Academy'. Let us note then, in passing, that Cicero admits the claim of philosophy, so far as he understands it, to an important place in educational theory, but denies its complete practical adequacy; we shall see later how, in Quintilian, the rivalry between rhetoric and philosophy has developed and hardened into a quarrel in which Quintilian ranges himself definitely on the side of rhetoric. Readers of Virgil will remember how he, with youthful ardour, gave his allegiance to philosophy:

> Ite hinc, inanes rhetorum ampullae,
> Inflata rore non Achaico verba.
>
> . . . .

Nos ad beatos vela mittimus portus,
Magni petentes docta dicta Sironis,
Vitamque ab omni vindicabimus cura.

(*Catalepton*, 5.)

To the hour of his death in 43 B.C. Cicero refused to despair of the Republic. But his murder was a forcible enough reminder to the Roman world that the days of political liberty and of free speech were at an end. The coming of the Empire, while it left untouched the outer forms and much of the routine of public life, wrought profound changes in its inner spirit and cut at the very root of current educational theory. Even Horace, enlisted as champion of the new régime, cannot but cry despairingly:

Damnosa quid non imminuit dies?
Aetas parentum, peior avis, tulit
Nos nequiores mox daturos
Progeniem vitiosiorem.

(*Odes*, iii. 6.)

When the benevolence of Augustus gave place to the sinister political uncertainty of the reigns of Tiberius and Nero, men might well ask of what use it was to train an orator for public service, if the opportunity to serve was denied him. Surely eloquence must be the most dangerous of gifts at the court of a despot; the best that a man can do is to keep quiet like Agricola and discharge with loyal care those military and administrative tasks which come his way. Such was the natural view, and there were many who endorsed it. On the other hand, there were still young people to be educated; the schools existed and had developed their technique, and they went on teaching with rhetoric as the main element in their higher instruction. After all, men had plenty of time, these days, to listen to declamations and displays of eloquence in the classroom and the lecture-hall, even if the senate no longer offered a safe field for oratory and public service.

Augustus lived to realize, in a father's bitter experience, that a return to the simpler ideals and austere morality of the earlier Republic was impossible. Education, which ever reflects the tone and temper of its age, soon assumed that artificiality which was the dominant feature of Roman public life in the early Empire. Oratory, driven from its sphere of public usefulness, focused its attention upon the cultivation of a style ever nicer and more minute, a kind of euphuism of which Seneca and Tacitus in prose, and Lucan in poetry, are supreme exponents. Men who might no longer study problems of statesmanship turned their genius to the study of words and phrases, to the fashioning of those epigrams with which the youthful Lucan and a dozen others delighted the jaded audiences of Rome. And now indeed rhetoric, divorced from real usefulness, became a dangerous thing; its influence upon Latin literature of the Silver Age is obvious; its prominence in the education of the early Empire was at once a sympton of unhealthiness and the cause of speedier corruption.

3. *Political and Social Environment of Quintilian's Teaching*

The pupils in Quintilian's school were boys and young men of wealth, and in some cases of noble birth. There was no question of preparing them for other careers than that of public service, either in the courts of law or in military commands or in civil administration. The task of the educator was made more difficult and his responsibility increased by the fact that the world into which these young men were to be launched was one of peculiar difficulty and danger. The trouble was that, while the political structure of the early Empire rested upon the personal ascendancy of the Emperor and in the last resort upon his military power, there was no recognized constitution, written or unwritten, to define his position in relation to the older elements in the state which still existed and were required to assist in the manifold tasks of government. In theory the Emperor was the chosen leader of the Roman people, dedicated to the service of the state and in virtue of his mission invested with divine attributes. In practice, a good Emperor, such as Marcus Aurelius, interpreted his functions very differently from a cruel and imperious autocrat like Domitian, and the whole atmosphere of life in Rome was coloured by the example of the reigning Emperor. It is not surprising then, that jealousy, misunderstanding, and sullen opposition should be constant factors in the political life of the age.

There were always many who felt that their claims to the Imperial purple were as strong as any one's, and the savage cruelty of the Terror was inspired by the fear of possible rivals. The natural desire of Augustus and his successors to establish the hereditary principle was opposed, not only by Stoic and Cynic theorists, but also by the deep-rooted prejudices of the Roman people. It is in this context that we must interpret Quintilian's coolness towards contemporary philosophy.

The bitterness of Vespasian's feud with the philosophers which led in the end to their expulsion from Rome, was due, on the one side, to the Emperor's determination to secure the accession of his sons, and, on the other, to the insistence of the opposition upon the adoptive principle in the selection of the best men for the task of leadership.

In the circumstances it is not surprising that Quintilian, who owed his official position to Vespasian and his successors, should have excluded from his curriculum a subject with such dangerous political implications as current philosophical speculation.

Such being the political environment, it is clear that the career of any one aspiring to public service was likely to be both difficult and dangerous, and that young men of equestrian or senatorial rank would be faced with temptations and trials of the utmost gravity.

Tacitus, in the sombre pages of the *Annals*, lets us see something of the conditions which had to be faced. He laments the weakness so often shown by men of noble birth, and contrasts with their degenerate cowardice the shining constancy of humbler folk in face of cruel persecution. But he hardly makes allowance for the demoralizing effect of the espionage which, under the baser and less scrupulous Emperors, formed a constant threat to the safety and tranquillity of life among the well-to-do in Rome. The infamous delatores throve upon the indiscretions or the innocent confidences of their hapless victims, and so men lived in an atmosphere of constant dread. This is the most demoralizing of experiences, and it is small wonder that nerve and moral courage should too often give way under the strain.

The religion of the day could offer no resources of spiritual comfort; Stoic philosophy might teach a man how to die, but not how to live. It was for education, as Quintilian saw, to build a type of character which would face these dangers serene and undismayed.

When we turn to the social environment of the youth of the early Empire, we are equally reminded of the significance of the words of Tacitus when he speaks of *infesta virtutibus tempora.* The social economy was based upon slavery which, even in the more benevolent form it assumed in Imperial times, implied an indifference to the value of human personality which was bound to react with fatal effect upon character and conduct. The sharp distinctions of class privilege which everywhere obtained mocked the philosophic doctrine of the brotherhood of man, as it might be preached by a Dio Chrysostom or an Epictetus.

The tradition of senatorial exclusiveness lived on long after senatorial power had dwindled to a shadow, and it was in no small measure injured pride which lent bitterness to the opposition under the earlier Caesars. The darkness of the social scene as pictured for us by Tacitus and Juvenal is in some measure relieved by the happier account of Roman aristocratic life given us in the letters of the younger Pliny.

From him we learn how tranquil and refined many homes remained in contrast with the hectic eccentricities of the Imperial court. The dullness of life in the provincial towns might invite the derision of the smart set in the capital, but the cult of country life, artificial as to some extent it was, showed how the strain of life in Rome was felt as an intolerable burden by all but the most hardened adventurers.

To feel the stifling atmosphere of life at court, we need only turn the pages of Seneca's *Dialogues*, in which he discourses with pathetic eloquence upon the

Brevity of Life and the Vanity of Human Wishes, and recall the tragic story of his career. How different is the spirit of the life lived by Pliny, whether in peaceful Comum or on the Emperor's business in Bithynia. The generosity which breathes through all his dealings with his native town is characteristic not only of Pliny but of very many others of his time, and nothing is more impressive in the records of the Empire than the mass of inscriptional evidence testifying to the local patriotism of such men as Pliny. It is clear that, in spite of all the vice and corruption which abounded in the great cities of the Empire, the life of the smaller provincial towns remained sound, and produced men, reared in the old tradition, who were proud to spend the wealth the Empire had brought them in the service of their fellow townsmen.

It was to this class that Vespasian himself belonged, and it was from this class that he drew the new nobility which, in his reign, brought fresh vitality to the Senate. Vespasian, a man of simple habits, brought to the society of the capital a new and healthier tone. Luxury and licence were frowned upon; economy and simplicity of life were encouraged by precept and example. With the coming of the Flavians a new era had dawned and there seemed some hope of a restoration of the ideals of the good old days of the Republic. Quintilian was in fullest sympathy with the old-fashioned virtues, and his appointment to the official Chair of Rhetoric was no doubt an item in the Emperor's programme of social reform. His striking popularity, even in aristocratic circles, is proof that the old Roman qualities of discipline and self-sacrifice could still arouse an echo in the hearts of many who would fain have their children taught to reverence and to practise them. In all classes there appeared an almost pathetic belief in the value of education, and an eagerness to extend its blessings as widely as possible. Let us now consider how Quintilian and his colleagues proposed to accomplish their task.

4. *Quintilian's Theory*

When Quintilian embarked on the writing of his great work, he had learned by experience the dangers of an oratory divorced from public service, and it is not an unfair view to see in his book a protest against current practice in education and an attempt to recall his contemporaries in the teaching world to the older ideals and to the simpler methods of the Republic. His object is to recall the viewpoint and to recover the ideals of Cicero, his great master and model, with certain modifications, no doubt, in points where the practical experience of a teacher of more than twenty years' standing might correct the enthusiasm of a theoretical philosopher of education.

It was clearly in this reforming spirit that Quintilian framed his criticism of Seneca to whom, in his survey of great writers in *Book X* (i. 125 et seq.), he devoted more space than to any other author save only Cicero. His statements are explicit; he had found that the artificial style of Seneca had a dangerous fascination for his pupils, who in seeking to imitate him could only manage to copy his faults. He admits that Seneca has many excellences but insists that he also abounds in sweet vices. 'One could wish that he had written with his own genius but with another's judgement'; and again 'if he had not broken in pieces the massive structure of his subjects by overstraining and by far-fetched conceits, he would have won the unanimous applause of learned men instead of the admiration of callow youths'.

'It is a mode of oratory which is corrupted and broken by all sorts of vicious practices that I am striving to recall to more austere standards', writes Quintilian (*Inst. Or.* x. i. 125). It is in the same spirit of reform that he frames his indictment of the professed philosophers of his time, and refuses to admit their claim to control the ideals of education. He declares that they are for the most part shams: 'I would willingly concede that many of the old philosophers taught things honourable and lived in accordance with their own precepts, but now the name often cloaks great vices, and a long face, a mournful manner, and an unusual garb conceal the worst depravity of morals.' Again we are reminded that philosophers are even at the best unpractical men; Quintilian would have sympathized with Avidius Cassius, who was constrained to call Marcus Aurelius 'the philosophical old wife'. He asserts roundly:

'I would not have my orator a philosopher, since no other group of men has withdrawn farther from the duties of citizenship and from all the tasks of oratory. Which of the philosophers, indeed, has ever attended assiduously in the law-courts or won fame in public assemblies? Which of them has had practical experience of the administration of public affairs about which most of them are fond of lecturing us? The Roman I am training ought to be wise indeed but one who will prove his worth as a true citizen not in private discussion and debate but by practical experience and exertion.'

We have already seen that there were also good political reasons for our author's distrust of philosophers. In this matter he is voicing an opinion widely held among his fellow citizens of Rome and expressed by other writers. Ennius had put it thus:

Philosophari est mihi necesse, at paucis; nam omnino haud placet.
Degustandum ex ea, non in eam ingurgitandum censeo.

Tacitus, speaking of Agricola, explains in apologetic vein:

'I remember how he used himself to say that in early life he was inclined to drink more deeply of philosophy than is permitted to a Roman senator, but being checked by his mother's discretion, achieved that hardest of feats, was a student and yet preserved his balanced outlook.'

Quintilian, then, is at one with very many of his fellow Romans when he insists upon practical training for his pupils; that his aims were not narrowly utilitarian will be manifest when we examine the general curriculum which he proposed for them. This is to be found in the first two books of the *Institutio*, the remainder of the work being devoted in the main to rhetoric, the subject or rather group of subjects which Quintilian had himself taught. In the twelfth and last book we find an account of the finished product as Quintilian would like him to be, the *vir vere civilis*, armed at every point for the service of his fellows.

(*a*) *Elementary Instruction.*

Quintilian begins by affirming the supreme importance of elementary education, the foundation upon which the whole superstructure must rest.

The development of his ideal pupil is to be watched and guided from infancy. Petrarch, in one of his *Letters to Dead Authors*, addresses Quintilian thus: 'thou dost lead thy future orator through all the turns and pitfalls of the long journey from the cradle to the impregnable citadel of eloquence.'

Nurses and tutors, then, must be chosen with care and a due regard for moral character and correctness of speech; it will be remembered that Philip of Macedon chose Aristotle to impart to his son Alexander the first rudiments of learning.

The first medium of instruction for our Roman pupil should be Greek; the reasons given for this are interesting. In the first place, Latin will be picked up in any case, because it is spoken by every one around our young charge. The same principle prescribes French in some English nurseries. The second reason adduced by Quintilian is that Greek comes before Latin in the work of the grammar school, and our Roman studies are derived from and dependent upon Greek. Latin should follow at no great interval, however, and the two languages should be continued side by side.

Formal instruction some would not begin before the age of seven; but Chrysippus held, and Quintilian agrees, that we may start earlier provided that we do not place any grievous burden upon tender minds or exact too close application. 'Let this first instruction be in the form of play', says our author, 'for one thing above all is to be guarded against, viz. that one who cannot yet love studies should come to hate all learning'. The idea of the Kindergarten is thus foreshadowed (i. 1. 20).

Next comes the question of school or private tuition.

Some parents argue that morals are corrupted at school, and also hold that individual attention from a tutor is superior to the mass methods of a class. Quintilian, however, points out that the defects of a school training are far outweighed by its positive advantages. Isolation produces apathy, conceit, or nervous shyness; school life is a social education; healthy rivalry is the best incentive to effort at this stage, and the teacher too finds inspiration in a larger audience (i. 2).

At the elementary school, then, the pupil will acquire a knowledge of reading, writing, and easy arithmetic (i. 3).

Corporal punishment is the next question discussed by Quintilian. Here he rejects the general practice of his times, condemning such punishment as degrading, ineffective, unnecessary if proper supervision is exercised, and liable to gross abuse in unworthy hands. Montaigne, in one of his *Essays* (Book I, Chap. 25), refers to this passage with approval, saying:

'I could never away with this kind of discipline used in most of our colleges. It had peradventure been less hurtfull if they had somewhat inclined to mildness or gentle intreatie. Come upon them when they are going to their lesson and you heare nothing but whipping and brawling both of children tormented and masters besotted with anger and chafing. How wide are they which go about to allure a child's mind to go to his booke, being yet but tender and fearefull, with a stearne-frowning countenance and with hands full of rods? O wicked and pernicious manner of teaching which Quintilian hath very well noted, that this imperious kind of authoritie, namely this way of punishing children, draws many dangerous inconveniences within. How much more decent were it to see their schoolhouses and formes strewed with greene boughs and flowers than with bloudy burchen-twigs.' (Florio's translation.)

As against corporal punishment Quintilian states true incentives to industry as being competition, commendation, affection for the teacher, interest aroused by the subject of study.

In this chapter (i. 3), which deals with the psychology of the class-room, we have our author at his best. He insists that the teacher must recognize and allow for differences of temperament and of intellectual gifts in different pupils, and that he must treat each pupil in the way best suited to his case. The strong emphasis here laid upon the individuality of the pupil and the close psychological observation revealed in the building up of a reasoned system of training are peculiar to Quintilian among Roman educators and to his strongly defined personality as a teacher. The average child, he insists, is intelligent and eager for knowledge, and it is the fault of his training if he ceases to be so; the main purpose of education is to foster mental activity.

But relaxation too is necessary. Games have their place in Quintilian's scheme, not as an end in themselves but as a means to increased efficiency. His words are significant:

'. . .nor should I be displeased by a love of play in my pupils, for this too is a sign of alertness, nor could I hope that a pupil who is always sombre and downcast would show keenness of mind in his studies; only let there be moderation in their recreations so that, on the one hand, refusal to allow them may not breed hatred of studies, and on the other, indulgence to excess may not foster the love of idleness.'

Moreover, games sharpen the wits and are a valuable

index of character; the wise teacher will study his pupils on the playing-field as well as in the class-room.

This passage on games has brought upon Quintilian the charge of over-intellectualism and a failure to understand the importance of bodily fitness as an end in itself. In reality he is protesting against the habits of his day, the endless time wasted on the Campus and at the Baths, the frittering away of energy which could be so much better employed in study, for youth, he reminds us, is the age best fitted to endure fatigue. Elsewhere (i. 12. 8) it is pointed out that the youthful mind and body have amazing powers of recuperation, and can stand more hard work than those of older men. The psychology of this is explained and the interesting point made that in study the youthful pupil does not estimate the difficulty of his task at any stage, and so is not affected, as the older student is, by the consciousness that effort is required: 'as we know by experience, the consciousness that exertion is required tells upon us more than the actual exertion itself' (i. 12. 11).

(*b*) *School of the Grammaticus.*

From the elementary school our pupil passes to the school of the grammaticus. This is the middle stage of his education in which the range of his interests is widened to include all the subjects which form the 'cycle of studies' recognized in the practice of Greek and Roman schools. This curriculum included grammar, composition and essay-writing, music, mathematics, physical and vocal training.

'Grammar' originally meant the study of the great poets, historians, and orators as literature, but tended more and more to include grammar in our sense of the term. The process is familiar enough; in the first instance, 'grammar' was simply an aid to the understanding of great books, but later the books became the happy hunting-ground in which the grammarian ran his facts to earth. Quintilian gives us a full account of the responsibilities of the grammaticus, for he is clearly convinced that 'grammar' is the foundation of higher education.

This was the view of the humanists of the Renaissance, and it is interesting to note that the charter of the Manchester Grammar School sets it forth thus: 'the liberal science or art of grammar is the ground and fountain of all the other liberal arts or sciences which source and spring out of the same; without which science the others cannot perfectly be had, for Science of Grammar is the Gate by the which all the other hath been learned and known.'

Recognizing the distinction between grammatical and literary studies, Quintilian devotes a very important chapter in Book I to showing how interesting the study of what we call grammar can be made. It is a passage of the greatest significance in the development of the science of language. On the literary side, our author's scheme represents the practice general in his time and familiar to us as the method in vogue in our own study of classical authors, 'exposition of the poets', scansion, study of figures of speech, explanation of difficult words and allusions, and criticism of the comparative kind. It will be remembered that Greek authors bulked largely in the programme of these classes in 'grammar', though by Quintilian's time Virgil's *Aeneid* and the works of Horace supplied a worthy counterpart in Latin to Homer and Greek Tragedy, and what was analogous to our modern language study had made great headway.

The expounding of texts which brought the child into the presence of great literary masterpieces was the central point from which all the work of the school of the grammaticus started and to which it all returned. Its effectiveness depended upon the personality of the teacher and his ability to inspire his pupils with something of his own enthusiasm. Hence the importance of choosing a good man for the task.

Hence, too, the fame of certain masters who, though lacking in dignity and polish, commanded respect by reason of their professional qualities and gifts. It was not enough to convey an understanding of the thoughts of the authors studied or even to encourage pupils to think for themselves. The real purpose of this minute study of the great writers was to rouse the mind, to impart a sense of style, and finally to cultivate the power of self-expression. And this brings us to the second subject in the curriculum of the grammaticus, the subject of composition in prose and verse.

'Expression', says Quintilian (viii, prooem. 16), 'is the main object of instruction; that is what art alone can give us, that ought to engage our every effort, the end of all our exercises and of our imitation, the work of our entire life.' The best pupil was the one who could write and speak best. The tombstone of a youthful scholar bears this touching expression of his dream of a great future: 'What hopes I might have afforded if destiny had permitted me to live, for the Muse had granted me, and that when I was still a child, the gift of eloquence.' True to their practical genius, the Romans saw in study an instrument and demanded of it a useful end, the end of 'eloquence'. This does not come fortuitously; it is only by continuous cultivation that it can develop. Hence the passionate interest in literary composition displayed by teachers and scholars alike in the period with which we are concerned. The results were astonishing, especially in the writing of poetry, in which the mind finds expression in the most beautiful and harmonious forms. Thanks to their study of the Greek masterpieces, Roman teachers had come to recognize that poetry and the work of the imagination are best fitted to mould the spirit and to afford that general intellectual training which the future orator must have. And so we find Virgil writing the *Culex* at the age of sixteen, Lucan composing his *Iliacon* at fourteen or fifteen, Ovid reading his first poem in public 'when his beard was just beginning to sprout'. It was not by teachers of narrow utilitarian views that these young poets were encouraged to produce such work.

The other subjects in the curriculum of the grammar school are definitely subordinate.

Music had a traditional place in education owing to Greek theory and practice, but as a theoretical study it made little appeal to Roman teachers. Quintilian is content to point out its practical value to the orator in the management of his voice and in his bodily movements.

He also indicates his agreement with Aristotle as to the moral value of strong manly strains, and protests against the effeminate and enervating music of the stage.

Mathematics, including arithmetic, geometry, and

astronomy, is of practical use as well as being a valuable logical training, an aspect which Quintilian readily recognizes.

Physical and vocal training are included in the curriculum, not to produce actors or professional athletes, but to impart grace and elegance of bearing and speech. The practices of the Greek wrestling-schools never commended themselves to serious Roman thinkers. In Quintilian's reference to them we hear a note of contempt which is rare in his work.

He speaks of 'teachers of gymnastic who give up part of their lives to anointing themselves with oil for wrestling and part to excessive drinking of wine, men who destroy the mind by too much attention to the body'. The tone is almost that of a Stoic philosopher; there is a similar passage in one of Seneca's letters in which he speaks of athletes as men *inter oleum et vinum occupati*, a phrase which may have been in Quintilian's mind. Nowhere is our author's divergence from Greek educational ideals more obvious than in his discussion of this question of athletic training. We can imagine how impatient his comment would have been on the training till recently in vogue for the Oxford and Cambridge boat-race or on the worship of athletics in some of our schools, where 'to the fourth-form boy the captain of the school Eleven is a far more awe-inspiring figure than the Headmaster' (Hon. Geo. Lyttelton).

Such then is the curriculum of the middle or grammar school, grammar (including literature), composition, music, mathematics, elocution, and physical training. This 'cycle of studies' did not rest upon any balanced theory of education; it was simply the sum-total of those branches of knowledge which the public demanded and in that respect resembled most systems of popular education. Quintilian accepts the scheme, and refers the value of each item in it to the practical test, its usefulness in moulding the perfect orator.

Before passing to the third stage, that of the school of rhetoric, our author devotes a chapter to the question whether the curriculum of the grammar school is overloaded. Here again we have a piece of psychological discussion of the greatest value. In answering the question in the negative Quintilian makes these points. First, concentration for long upon a single subject is difficult; *varietas animos reficit*, change of occupation rests and refreshes the mind, as change of diet rests the digestion. Again, the mind is more receptive before it hardens and sets, so that a child learns to speak Latin in two years, whereas an adult slave brought to Rome wrestles with the language for many. Try to teach an adult to read and you will appreciate the reason for calling those who excel in their own arts 'paidomatheis', that is to say, learners in youth. Finally, there will never be more time for study than there is in this receptive period of adolescence when the critical judgement is not yet fully awake. The real fact is that we make the plea of difficulty and over-pressure a cloak for our own laziness; we do not seek education for the sake of divine eloquence herself but for selfish gain, which we would fain secure without unnecessary and fatiguing accomplishments.

Here we have the plea for a liberal education of a sufficiently general type as against entrance at too early a stage upon the specialized study of rhetoric and declamation. The point is made more clearly still by Tacitus, writing a little earlier than Quintilian, in his

Dialogue on Orators: 'I pass by the first rudiments of education, though even these are taken too lightly; it is in the reading of authors and in gaining a knowledge of the past, and in making acquaintance with things and persons and occasions that too little solid work is done. Recourse is had instead to the so-called rhetoricians.' In applying the idea to our own times we might paraphrase it in the form: 'recourse is had instead to the business college and the school of technology.' 'Contrast', he goes on to say, 'the education of Cicero as we read of it in the *Brutus*; it is from a wealth of learning, a multitude of accomplishments, and a knowledge that is universal that his marvellous eloquence wells forth like a mighty stream' (Tacitus, *Dialogus*, 30). We are reminded of the definition of education as what is left when you have forgotten everything you have learnt.

(*c*) *School of Rhetoric*.

The training of the grammar school then should be of a general type; we pass from it to the specialized training of the school of rhetoric.

There is no definite age, says Quintilian, for the change; it should come when the pupil is ready for it, normally at thirteen or fourteen, which, if we allow for southern conditions, would correspond to fifteen or sixteen with us. Care must be taken not to allow declamation to encroach upon the work of the grammar school.

In the school of rhetoric, as in the school of the grammaticus, the personality of the teacher is all-important. The qualities to be looked for are high moral character, power of clear exposition, patience, and generosity. He must have ability and learning as well; in fact, he must have all the gifts of Phoenix the tutor of Achilles.

The pupil, for his part, will remember that his teacher is the parent not of his body, but of his mind, and will love him as he will love his studies. Such dutiful affection and mutual consideration will make the work of the school smooth and efficient.

The curriculum for this, the highest stage of Roman education, is set out by Quintilian as including (*a*) a further graduated course of exercises in composition, culminating in declamation which is universally regarded as the coping-stone of the educational structure; (*b*) reading of prose authors corresponding to the reading of the poets in the grammar school, with special attention to points of criticism; (*c*) lectures on the formal theory of rhetoric.

This, the formal work of the school, will be supplemented by a good deal of private reading and writing by the pupil, exercises in composition, translation from Greek, paraphrasing of passages from Latin authors, improvisation and revision.

The pupil is now at a stage where he can do a good deal for himself; but it is clear from the account we have in Book II of Quintilian's own methods, that he gave individual attention to his pupil's exercises and declamations. We do not know the number of his pupils, but it must have been considerable, and when we remember his responsibilities as an advocate and as a public declaimer, we cannot but admire his industry.

The absence of philosophy from the curriculum of Quintilian's school of rhetoric is noteworthy. We have seen how Cicero had postulated a philosophical training for his 'eloquent man'; and the whole tone of Quintilian's exposition, with its insistence on high moral character in teacher and pupil alike, together with his criticism of the bad influence of much of the home life of the Imperial period, would lead us to look for some training in ethical theory at least somewhere in the curriculum. The fact seems to be that Quintilian refuses to include a subject or group of subjects which had come to be identified in practice with abstention from public life, and in the case of the two most popular creeds, Stoicism and Cynicism, with opposition to the hereditary principle in the Imperial succession. This political implication of current philosophy was the main reason for the expulsion of the philosophers in A.D. 71–74 by Vespasian, and again about A.D. 94 by Domitian. The action of these Emperors was no mere act of wanton tyranny; it had the support of a considerable body of responsible public opinion and doubtless Quintilian, who was at all times a loyal servant of the reigning Emperor, gave it his hearty approval.

Such an attitude was by no means inconsistent with the admiration he expresses for the older philosophers and their work. His general position would seem to be that the teacher of rhetoric is himself so saturated in philosophical principles that he cannot fail to convey their spirit to his pupils, but that he must not allow pure philosophy to cloud the vision of practical service which is to be our youthful orator's inspiration, or tempt him to identify himself with any one of the philosophical schools. We have already (p. xxi) seen what his general attitude was and how he is in this matter in accord with many of his fellow citizens.

He sums the matter up thus: 'in studying the philosophers we must use our judgement and remember that the same manner is not suited to lawsuits and to philosophical disputations, to the forum and to the lecture-room, to exercises on rules and to actual trials' (x. 1. 35–6).

The normal practice at Rome was apparently that, if a special course in philosophy was taken at all, it was after the completion of the course in the school of rhetoric. But this is not recommended by Quintilian; he would send his pupils straight into practical life, and the course of reading in philosophy recommended in xii. 2 would in the author's view be a matter of private study either during or after the rhetorical course, like the reading of history and law which he also suggests.

The case for a knowledge of law and jurisprudence as part of the equipment of the would-be orator is an obvious one.

More interesting is Quintilian's attitude to the study of history. There is no indication of a serious and methodical study of history in the Roman schools. It was regarded rather as a convenient store-house of illustrations for use in speeches, and the declamations which have come down to us make this clear. In a well-known passage in the tenth book, history is described as 'the branch of literature nearest to poetry, a kind of prose poem, written to tell a story and not to prove a case'. On the other hand, we find Cicero describing history as pre-eminently an orator's work. Neither statement would satisfy the modern scientific historian; what is really meant in both statements is that the writing of history is no mere chronicling of events, but the task of a literary artist. Whilst we may admit that to give life to the past is a task of difficulty and that the power to do it is the most precious of gifts, we cannot be blind to the dangers of an attitude which would tolerate the modification of historical facts to suit the exigencies of story-telling or rhetoric. It is Cicero himself who says; 'when the rhetor invokes history, it is not forbidden him to lie in order to give more point to what he has to say'.

We must now return to the declamations which form so important an element in the training given in the school of rhetoric. They were of two types, 'suasoriae' and 'controversiae.'

The 'suasoria' is a dramatic monologue put into the mouth of some well-known historical personage. Thus, for example, Sulla deliberates whether he will give up his dictatorship, or again, Cicero debates with himself whether he will apologize to Antony and so save his life. The poet Persius tells us that, when he was a small boy, he rubbed his eyes with oil in order that, on the plea of their soreness, he might escape school and the dreariness of listening to a batch of youthful Catos soliloquizing before their suicide.

The 'controversia' was more elaborate and difficult. It was a mock trial in which pupils acted as prosecutors, defendants, and advocates. In earlier times these imaginary cases were of a practical type.

There was, for example, the case of the young man at Ostia who bought the catch of some fishermen in advance. When the net was pulled up, no fish were found in it, but a box of gold to which both parties laid claim. Or again, slave-dealers, to defraud the customs, deck out a valuable slave in a purple embroidered toga and put a golden bulla about his neck; in Rome the fraud is detected and the freedom of the boy demanded, on the ground that the action of the dealers is a renunciation of ownership.

But soon such practical issues were ousted by imaginary cases of a more sensational and unreal type, in which the tyrant, the pirate, and, later, the magician became the central figures. A favourite case was that of the young man who, to gain his freedom, marries the pirate's daughter; his own father, wishing to marry him to a wealthy orphan, calls upon him to renounce his pirate bride; he refuses and is himself repudiated. In many cases there was a strenuous and painful conflict between equally binding obligations. For example, in a civil war, a woman has her father and brother on one side, her husband on the other. She follows the latter, who is killed, and then returns for refuge to her father who spurns her. 'How shall I appease you?' she cries. 'Die!' Whereupon she hangs herself at his door and the son proposes that his father be declared insane.

In the collection bearing Quintilian's name, there is an excellent example of the well-known 'enchanted tomb' controversia. A mother, who has lost her son, is visited nightly by his ghost in her dreams. She tells her husband and he gets a magician to cast a spell over the tomb. The nightly visitations cease, whereupon the wife brings an action against her husband 'on the ground of ill-treatment'.

Such were the cases upon which the pupils of the schools of rhetoric exercised their ingenuity and wit, amid the thunderous applause of fellow students and fond parents, who listened 'in perspiring ecstasy'.

The weaknesses of such exercises in declamation have been emphasized by critics ancient and modern. Juvenal jeers at the hackneyed and sensational themes:

occidit miseros crambe repetita magistros (*Sat.* vii. 154).

Petronius emphasizes the same point in the first extant chapter of his *Satyricon*:

'I think that the youths in our schools become absolute fools because they hear and see nothing of real life, but only pirates standing in chains on the sea-shore, or tyrants writing edicts commanding sons to cut off their fathers' heads, or oracular responses in time of plague ordering the sacrifice of three or more maidens, the whole thing described in honeyed periods, all drenched in poppy and sesame. Pupils trained in such an atmosphere cannot possibly develop common sense, any more than those who live in a kitchen can smell sweet!'

Tacitus, in the *Dialogus*, contrasts the foolish bombast and the remoteness from life of the themes and methods of schools of rhetoric with the practical training of the young orator in the days of the Republic, and attributes the decline in eloquence largely to the changed outlook in education.

Quintilian was not unaware of the criticisms to which declamations were exposed. He tells us that parents were foolishly eager to hear their children declaim as often as possible, and took no interest in other parts of school work; hence a tendency for declamation to absorb nearly the whole of a pupil's time at school. But if this tendency is resisted, there is no reason why the great value of a sound training in the art of public speaking should not be realized.

While we smile at the well-worn themes and the conventional figures which so constantly occupied these young declaimers, let us not forget all that this training implies. There must be a clear understanding of a wide range of legal and other technical terms, a correct and intelligent use of language, a proper sense of the value of words, which convey our ideas. The declaimer must also have his memory stored with fine passages, for it is by familiar intercourse with the work of the great masters that we make ourselves in turn more or less capable of thinking fine thoughts. The elder Seneca said of oratory that it trains men not merely for declamation but for the whole of life, and in the case of a great teacher like Quintilian this was true. The obvious danger of developing sophistical brilliance rather than solidity of mind, of cultivating the imagination at the expense of reason and good sense, was less in the case of the practical Roman student than it had been in that of the more subtle-minded Greeks.

5. *Elements of Permanent Value in his Doctrine*

In our analysis of Quintilian's theory we have already illustrated his grasp of the psychological principles which underlie the practice of the class-room. It remains to consider in more general terms his contribution to the development of educational thought.

So far as the content of his curriculum was concerned, he was no innovator; he accepted the current practice and the 'cycle of studies' common to the schools of the day. His success as a teacher was mainly due to the sweet reasonableness of his nature and his untiring devotion to the welfare of his pupils. 'Let us pretend', he says, 'that it is Alexander (i.e. Alexander the Great) who is committed to our charge, a child worthy of infinite care, though every man thinks that of his own child' (*Inst. Or.* i. 1. 24).

The value of the pupil as an individual personality and the need to respect his individuality are points stressed by Quintilian many times and must be regarded as among the most important lessons he has to teach us. But what distinguishes him from his fellows and remains as something of lasting value to all educators of whatever age, is his insistence upon the moral value to the community of a liberal education. Like Fronto, the tutor of Marcus Aurelius, Quintilian was convinced that eloquence was the greatest power in human life, and that the training of the perfect orator was the supreme task of education. To accomplish this he was not content with merely technical training but aimed at imparting to his pupils all that is implied in the word *humanitas*. In a famous passage in the first chapter of Book X our author gives a sketch of the authors, both Greek and Latin, whom he would have his pupils read. Students of literary criticism have found some of the pronouncements here made disappointing, but for our purpose the great value of the passage lies in its revelation of the range and quality of the reading which Quintilian regards as necessary for the building up of *copia rerum ac verborum* in the budding orator. It includes poetry, the drama, history, oratory, and philosophy, covering the whole range of humane letters in both Greek and Latin, and amply testifying to Quintilian's belief in a wide liberal training. 'Humane' or 'liberal' studies alone possess that openness of spirit, that liveliness of sympathy, that knowledge of the human heart, that love of the beautiful, which raise man above his instincts and establish his dignity. Cicero, whom Quintilian revered, had expounded this thesis, and had brought into use this word *humanitas*, which designated not only certain studies but civilization itself; they had grown under the same influence and gave each other mutual support. As has been well said, 'the humanities and letters are man himself; to remove them from education, it would be necessary to commence by taking man from man'. This was a lesson which the schools of Rome had learnt from Greece, and which in turn they handed on to the scholars of the Renaissance. Its influence was all-pervasive. It enriched the Latin language and literature; it transformed the spirit of Roman family life; it rationalized law and political theory; it brought with it a science of morals which enabled virtue to find its strength in conscience rather than in tradition. And in our own more complex conditions of life, when so strong a case can be made out for 'useful' studies, it is a doctrine we must not forget. The spirit of man will always find its true nourishment in those liberal arts which concern themselves with the things of the spirit, and in the final assessment our schools will be counted great according to their power in fostering a love of the 'humanities', the term being understood in its widest connotation.

Complementary to Quintilian's belief in the value of a 'liberal' training which will nourish the imagination and the spirit is his insistence upon the training of the will, the building of character.

The product of his system of training is to be none other than the 'good man, skilled in speaking', in whom, two hundred years earlier, Marcus Cato had seen the perfect orator. To this, the moral aspect of education, Quintilian devotes his twelfth and last book, in which he elaborates the thesis that the product of our educational system must be the good man. To those who regard rhetoric as an artificial thing, insincere in its very nature, Whately's judgement that Quintilian's claim is 'fantastic' will commend itself. Instances will at once come to mind of great orators whose moral character has not been above reproach; Quintilian himself quotes Demosthenes and Cicero, the two greatest orators of antiquity, as incurring blame on moral grounds. His answer to the criticism is twofold. In the first place, the charges made against them have been exaggerated, and in the second, admitting that some of these charges were true, we recognize that so far they fell short of the ideal we are striving to realize. Even if Demosthenes and Cicero fell short of perfection, we must continue to aim at it, hoping that some day we may send forth a pupil who will reach the heights, and assured meanwhile that our high ideal will have its effect upon the whole body of our scholars. It is the spirit of true service which we must foster in our *vir vere civilis*, our pupil who, thrice armed by the consciousness of his own high purpose will stand forth to serve his country, like the patriot in Virgil's picture:

> ac veluti magno in populo cum saepe coorta est
> seditio, saevitque animis ignobile volgus,
> iamque faces et saxa volant, furor arma ministrat;
> tum, pietate gravem ac meritis si forte virum quem
> conspexere, silent arrectisque auribus astant;
> ille regit dictis animos et pectora mulcet.
>
> (Virg. *Aen.* i. 148–53.)

Here too we may recognize a permanent contribution to educational thought, in which the practical moral sense of the Roman teacher is blended with the idealism of his Greek predecessors. If Quintilian never rises to the heights of genius, if his style falls short of great eloquence, yet he never loses his gift of sanity and practical wisdom.

His qualities are those of good judgement, good taste, and good sense. We cannot afford to neglect this representative figure in Roman education, who has not only told us far more than any other writer about Roman methods and Roman ideals, but has also, as the fruits of his innate wisdom and long experience, left to his successors a body of sound doctrine, entitling him to an honoured place in the history of educational theory and practice.

Though much of the actual curriculum with which Quintilian is concerned seems strange to modern readers and out of touch with modern educational conditions, yet the student who is prepared to use his imagination and to make the necessary adjustments to our own subjects of study and to our very different environment will be able to discern in Quintilian's exposition a wise and balanced statement of principles which are of abiding value to all who are concerned with the psychology and practice of education. This cannot be better expressed than in the words of J. W. Mackail who sums up his brilliant survey of Quintilian's contribution to educational theory and practice in the following passage:

'Almost for the first time in history—for the ideal system of Plato, however brilliant and suggestive, stands on quite a different footing—the theory of education was, in this age, made a subject of profound thought and study. The precepts of Quintilian, if taken in detail, address themselves to the formation of a Roman of the Empire, and not a citizen of modern Europe. But their main spirit is independent of the accidents of any age or country. In the breadth of his ideas, and in the wisdom of much of his detailed advice, Quintilian takes a place in the foremost rank of educational writers. The dialogue on oratory written a few years earlier by Tacitus names as the main cause of the decay of the liberal arts, not any lack of substantial encouragement, but the negligence of parents and the want of skill in teachers. To leave off vague and easy declamations against luxury and the decay of morals, and to fix on the great truth that bad education is responsible for bad life, was the first step towards a real reform. This Quintilian insists upon with admirable clearness. Nor has any writer on education grasped more firmly or expressed more lucidly the complementary truth that education, from the cradle upwards, is something which acts on the whole intellectual and moral nature, and whose object is the production of what the Romans called, in a simple form of words which was full of meaning, "the good man".' (J. W. Mackail, *Latin Literature*, pp. 200–1.)

6. *Quintilian's Influence upon Some Later Writers*

To the Humanists of the Renaissance Quintilian commended himself partly by his advocacy of liberal studies, and partly by his insistence upon practical skill in his ideal orator. The influence he exercised over these scholars is amazing; his ideal suited exactly an age in which the demand for qualities of leadership was paramount. For them, as for him, the purpose of education was to train citizens, fully equipped in intellect and character.

Petrarch shows more discrimination in his praise than

do some of the later Humanists, and, in his 'Letter to Quintilian', says shrewdly enough: 'thou hast performed the office of the whetstone rather than that of the knife, and thou hast had greater success in building up the orator than in causing him to excel in the courts; thou wert a great man, I grant, but thy greatest merit lay in thy ability to ground and to mould great men.' (Cozenza's translation.) His verdict is that Quintilian is greater as an educator than as a stylist or an orator.

It was only a mutilated text to which Petrarch had access; the discovery of the complete text of the *Institutio* in 1416 was hailed as a great event. Scholars like Laurentius Valla and Politianus ranked Quintilian close to, if not above, Cicero. Vittorino da Feltre seems to have steeped himself in our author and to have been regarded by his contemporaries and successors as a kind of Quintilianus *redivivus*.

Erasmus knew his Quintilian from end to end, and built up his own work on education on that foundation.

Luther mentions Quintilian only once, but in arresting terms. In a letter he says: 'I assure you I prefer Quintilian to almost all other authorities (on education), for while he teaches he also gives us a model of eloquence, i.e. he teaches by the happiest combination of theory and practice.'

In the sixteenth century it appears that the chair of Rhetoric at Leipzig was held by a 'professor Quintiliani' instead of by the more usual 'professor eloquentiae'.

These instances, taken from many, will serve to illustrate the great popularity of Quintilian among continental Humanists. In England he never commanded such esteem.

Elyot, in his *Governour* (1531), and Richard Mulcaster show knowledge of his work; Roger Ascham in the *Schoolmaster* (1570) quotes him without enthusiasm.

Ben Jonson in his *Discoveries* includes a considerable adaptation of Quintilian. It was not realized by the earlier critics that the *Discoveries* was a commonplace book of Ben Jonson's, and in consequence, they criticize the views expressed in it as though they were his own.

Swinburne fell into this trap, and we have from his pen the following comment on the sections of the *Discoveries* which were really translated from Quintilian: 'If the nineteenth century has said anything on this subject as well worth hearing, as wise, as humane, as full of sympathy and judgement as these reflections and animadversions of a scholar of the first half or quarter of the seventeenth, I have not chanced to meet it.'

Pope knew and appreciated Quintilian, who was in many ways in tune with our own eighteenth century. The reference in the Essay on Criticism is well-known:

> in grave Quintilian's copious work we find
> the justest rules and clearest methods joined;
> thus useful arms in magazines we place
> all ranged in order and dispos'd with grace,
> but less to please the eye than arm the hand
> still fit for use and ready at command.

Elsewhere in the Essay Quintilian is paraphrased, e.g.

> some by old words to fame have made pretence,
> ancients in phrase, mere moderns in their sense;
> such laboured nothings, in so strange a style,
> amaze the unlearn'd, and make the learned smile.

This, as Pope himself tells us, is an amplification of Quintilian's 'abolita et abrogata retinere insolentiae cuiusdam est, et frivolae in parvis iactantiae' (i. 6. 20).

Finally John Stuart Mill, writing in his *Autobiography* of his reading at the age of twelve, says: 'Quintilian is little read and seldom sufficiently appreciated. His book is a kind of encyclopaedia of the thoughts of the ancients on the whole field of education and culture; and I have retained through life many valuable ideas which I can distinctly trace to my reading of him, even at that early age.'

For further illustrations of Quintilian's influence upon later writers the student is referred to F. H. Colson's edition of Book I of the *Institutio* (Cambridge, 1924), to which much of the information in this section is due. Reference may also be made to an article in the *Classical Review* of March 1907, in which W. H. S. Jones discusses the relation of Quintilian to the classical revival.

7. *Some Authorities consulted*

APPEL, B. *Das Bildungs- und Erziehungsideal Quintilians nach der Institutio Oratoria*, Donauwörth, 1914.

BARBAGALLO, CORRADO. *Lo Stato e l'Istruzione Pubblica nell'Impero Romano*, Catania, 1911.

BOISSIER, GASTON. *Tacitus and other Roman Studies*, translated by W. G. Hutchison, Constable, 1906.

COLSON, F. H. *Quintiliani Institutio Oratoria*, Book I, Cambridge University Press, 1924.

DILL, SAMUEL. *Roman Society from Nero to Marcus Aurelius*, Macmillan, 1905.

GWYNN, AUBREY. *Roman Education from Cicero to Quintilian*, Oxford University Press, 1926.

HULSEBOS, G. A. *De Educatione et Institutione apud Romanos*, Traiecti ad Rhenum, 1867.

JULLIEN, ÉMILE. *Les Professeurs de Littérature dans l'ancienne Rome*, Paris, 1885.

LAURIE, S. S. *Historical Survey of Pre-Christian Education*, Longmans, 1895.

MACKAIL, J. W. *Latin Literature*, Murray, 1899.

ROSTOVTZEFF, M. *The Social and Economic History of the Roman Empire*, Oxford University Press, 1926.

SANDYS, J. *A History of Classical Scholarship*, vol. i (2nd ed.), Cambridge University Press, 1906.

WELLS, J., and BARROW, R. H. *A Short History of the Roman Empire* (2nd ed.), Methuen, 1935.

WILKINS, A. S. *Roman Education*, Cambridge University Press, 1905.

SELECTED PASSAGES FROM THE EDUCATION OF AN ORATOR

BY

MARCUS FABIUS QUINTILIANUS

PREFACE OR EPISTLE FROM THE AUTHOR TO HIS PUBLISHER

Quintilian to his friend Trypho, greeting

DAY by day with never-ending entreaty you have besought me to begin the publication of the volumes on the Training of an Orator dedicated by me to my friend Marcellus. My own feeling is that the work has not yet sufficiently matured, for on its composition, as you are aware, I have spent little more than two years, in spite of countless other occupations; and that time has been devoted not so much to actual writing as to the research involved by the almost limitless task I have undertaken and to the reading of innumerable authorities.

Then following the advice of Horace who in his Art of Poetry deprecates too hasty publication and urges that a work 'should not appear till nine years have elapsed', I intended to give my book a rest so that, after the too partial frenzy of composition had cooled off, I might revise it with more care and weigh its merits as a reader might.

But if there is really so eager a demand for the work as you say there is, let us set sail and pray for a blessing as we cast off from the shore. Much however depends upon your loyal care also, that the book may reach the public in as perfect a form as is possible.

BOOK I

INTRODUCTION

1. After I obtained a respite from the labours which for twenty years I had devoted to the education of the young, a friendly request came from certain quarters that I should write something on the principles of oratory, but for a long time I hung back knowing that very famous authors, both Greek and Roman, had left to posterity numerous writings dealing with the subject in the most thorough-going way.

2. But the plea which I thought would win me readier indulgence in my diffidence only served to kindle more enthusiasm amongst my friends, because, as they declared, it was a difficult matter to choose amid the contrasting views of earlier writers, views sometimes inconsistent with each other, and so they seemed justified in imposing on me the task, if not of writing something original, at any rate of passing judgement on what had already been written.

3. But, although my scruples were overcome not so much by confidence that I could do what was required of me as by shame at the thought of refusing to make the attempt, yet as the subject opened out more widely to my view I shouldered willingly a greater burden than that originally imposed upon me. My object in so doing was twofold, in the first place to oblige my dearest friends by a fuller compliance with their wishes and secondly, in travelling a familiar road, to avoid simply following in the footsteps of others.

4. For practically all previous writers on the art of pleading started by assuming that they were simply

adding the finishing touches in eloquence to pupils already perfect in every other branch of learning. They did so, either because they despised our preliminary studies as things of small importance or because they considered them outside their peculiar province in view of the specialized functions of the various departments of education or else, as is most likely, because they could not look for any enhancement of their reputation as men of genius in dealing with minutiae which, though necessary, are far from being showy—just as, in the case of buildings, the gables catch the eye, whilst the foundations are concealed.

5. But for my part, holding as I do first, that nothing is foreign to the art of oratory which must be admitted to be necessary for the making of an orator and second, that no one reaches the highest stages of a subject without passing through the initial stages which precede them, I shall not refuse to stoop to the consideration of those matters which are indeed of less importance but which if neglected preclude the possibility of advance to higher things, and I shall begin to mould the studies of the orator from infancy, as if his entire upbringing were committed to my care.

6. This work I dedicate to you, Victorius Marcellus, a very dear friend and a devoted lover of letters. Yet it is not because of these considerations only, weighty as they are, that I adjudged you in the highest degree worthy of this pledge of our mutual affection, it was also because it seemed likely that in the education of your son Geta, whose early years already reveal the clear light of genius, you would find a treatise useful in which my intention was to start from the very cradle, so to speak, of oratory, to deal successively with all the

studies which in any way contribute to the making of the orator, and to lead right up to the culmination of his art.

7. And I was the more anxious to compose the work because two books on the Art of Rhetoric had already appeared bearing my name but neither published by me nor put together for that purpose. One was a two days' discourse seized upon by the pupils to whom the time was devoted, the other was a reproduction, as far as notes permitted, of a course of lectures extending over a greater number of days, issued by youths whose well-meaning but excessive devotion sought to do me honour by premature publication.

8. Accordingly in the present volume there will be certain repetitions, many alterations and very many additions, and the whole subject will be presented in a more systematic fashion and in as finished a form as I can achieve.

9. It is the perfect orator that we are training and he cannot even exist unless he is a good man. We therefore demand in him not only exceptional powers of eloquence but also every mental excellence.

10. Nor indeed would I admit that the principles which underlie an upright and honourable life should be left to the philosophers, as some have thought; for the ideal citizen, fitted to take his share in the management of public and private affairs, able to govern cities by his wise counsels, to establish them upon a sure foundation of good laws and to improve them by the administration of impartial justice, is assuredly none other than the orator.

11. Wherefore, admitting that I will make use of certain principles which are to be found in the books of the

philosophers, I would none the less maintain that they truly and rightfully belong to our sphere and have a direct bearing on the Art of Oratory.

12. Or if it be found that we have to talk continually of justice, bravery, temperance, and the other virtues to such an extent that scarcely a single case can be found which does not involve some question of this kind, and if all these themes have to be set forth by means of constructive reasoning and lucid exposition, will it be doubted that wherever intellectual power and ready eloquence are demanded, there is the peculiar province of the orator?

13. These qualities, as Cicero very clearly shows, were not only joined by nature but also associated in practice, so that originally the same men were considered both wise and eloquent. Then this twofold study was divided and through lack of art it comes about that the arts appeared to be distinct. For as soon as the tongue became a source of gain, and men began to make an evil use of the good gift of eloquence, those who were considered fluent speakers abandoned the care of morals;

14. And being thus cast off it fell a prey, so to speak, to the feebler intellects. Then certain men, despising the toilsome pursuit of eloquence, fell back upon the moulding of the human mind and the establishment of laws to regulate the life of man; and thus they kept what was indeed the nobler part, if a division were possible, but assumed a totally unwarranted title by claiming for themselves alone the name of 'lovers of wisdom'. For neither the greatest generals nor those who played the most prominent parts in the weightiest counsels and in the administration of the Commonwealth dared to ad-

vance so preposterous a claim. They preferred to do the noblest deeds rather than to profess them.

15. I would willingly concede that many of the old professors of philosophy taught things honourable and lived in accordance with their own precepts. But in these our times the name has often cloaked great vices. In such cases philosophers did not make it the object of their labour through goodness and devotion to be considered 'lovers of wisdom' but sought rather to make a long face, a mournful manner, and an unusual garb conceal the worst depravity of morals.

16. Those topics which are claimed by the philosophers as exclusively their own are handled by every one of us continually. Who, unless he be the most depraved of men, does not speak of what is just, right, and good? What man even amongst our bumpkins does not make some inquiry into the causes of natural phenomena? while the proper use of words and their different meanings ought to be the common concern of all who care aught for human speech.

17. Yet all these matters will be best understood and exemplified by the orator. And, if a perfect orator had ever existed, the precepts of human excellence would not now be sought in the schools of the philosophers. As things are, it is sometimes necessary to refer to those authors who have seized upon what I have called the deserted portion of the art of oratory (and the better portion to boot), and as it were to reclaim our own, not that we may use their discoveries but in order to show that they have appropriated what is not theirs.

18. Let us then define the orator as a man who can truly be called wise, perfect not only in character (for in my opinion, though some think differently, that is not

enough) but also in knowledge and every sort of eloquence.

19. Such a man perhaps has never yet existed. But that is no reason why we should not strive towards the highest ideal, as was done by the ancients for the most part. For, although they considered that so far no wise man had been discovered, they none the less wrote down the precepts whereby wisdom might be attained.

20. Assuredly there is such a thing as perfect eloquence nor does the nature of the human intellect forbid its realization. And even if it never were attained, still those who strive towards the highest will reach greater heights than those who despair at the outset of ever reaching their ideal and stop short at the lowest levels.

21. For these reasons I shall be able to claim indulgence if I do not omit to deal even with those minor details which are none the less essential to my task.

The first book will deal with those branches of instruction which precede the rhetor's training.

In the second I shall treat of the elementary instruction of the rhetor's school and of the questions which arise concerning the subject-matter of rhetoric itself.

22. The next five books (III-VII) will be devoted to 'invention', i.e. constructive reasoning, with a subsection on arrangement, and four more (VIII-XI) to 'elocution', i.e. the practice of oratory, a section which includes memory and delivery.

There will be one book more (XII) in which I have to sketch the ideal orator in person. And here I shall discourse, as far as my feeble powers avail, upon the following topics—the character of the orator, the principles which guide him in undertaking, preparing, and pleading cases, the nature of eloquence, the time when pleading should cease, the pursuits of the orator when he retires from the bar.

23. Interspersed with these topics as occasion demands, will be found theoretical instruction not merely intended to supply the serious student with a knowledge of these technical points to which alone the name of art has been given by some, and if I may say so to expound the fundamental laws of rhetoric, but also fitted to nourish fluency of speech and to increase the power of eloquence.

24. As a rule these abstract treatises on the art of rhetoric, by striving after undue precision, blunt and shatter all the nobler part of oratory and drain the sap of the intellect, laying bare the bones which ought of course to exist and to be bound one to another by the sinews, but ought also to be covered with flesh and blood.

25. I have therefore embodied in these twelve books not simply that small portion with which most authors have been content, but everything which I considered useful for the training of the orator. In all cases the treatment will be brief for, if I were to follow out all that could be said in detail, my work would never end.

26. This axiom must be laid down at the very outset, that precepts and rules of art avail nothing unless nature lends her aid. This book is no more written for him who lacks natural ability than is a book on agriculture for barren soils.

27. There are also other aids to oratory inborn in different men, a good voice, a strong constitution, good health, strength of character, charm of manner. If these are present even in a moderate degree, they can be

developed by systematic training; sometimes their absence neutralizes the advantages even of natural ability and earnest study. On the other hand these very gifts without a skilled teacher, persevering application, and much continuous practice in writing, reading, and speaking, are in themselves of no avail.

CHAPTER 1

THE METHOD OF PRIMARY INSTRUCTION

1. WHEN his son is born, let the father first of all conceive the highest hopes concerning him, for so he will become more careful from the start.

There is no foundation in fact for the complaint that to very few is given the power of understanding what is taught them but that the majority waste both time and labour through slowness of intellect.

On the contrary, you can find many who are clever at puzzling things out and quick at learning. Indeed such aptitude is natural to man, and just as birds are born to fly, horses to run, and wild beasts to show fierceness, so our peculiar gift is mental activity and cleverness and for that reason the origin of mind is held to be divine.

2. But dullness and lack of aptitude for learning are no more in accordance with man's nature than are bodily abnormalities and deformity; they occur but seldom and the proof of it is this, that most men form high hopes of their sons; but when, as these sons grow older, such hopes fade away, clearly it is not nature that is at fault but human care.

'Still, one man does surpass another in natural ability.'

3. Granted; but even so he will accomplish more or less; for no one is found who has not profited at all by study.

Let him who has grasped this fact, as soon as he becomes a father, devote the keenest possible attention to the promise of the budding orator.

4. Before all things else, let the speech of his nurses be correct. Chrysippus wished them, if it were possible,

to be educated women, but at any rate he desired the best available to be selected. And of course in the case of nurses account must first be taken of moral character; still let them also speak correctly.

5. Theirs are the voices the child will hear first, theirs the words he will try to reproduce. And we are naturally most tenacious of what we learned while our minds were still unformed: as the flavour imparted to vessels when they are new remains in them and the colours of woollen stuffs wherewith their original whiteness has been transformed cannot be washed out.

And further those very impressions which are less desirable are the more enduring. Good things are easily changed for the worse, but when will you turn vices into virtues? Do not then allow the boy, even in infancy, to become familiar with a way of speaking which has afterwards to be unlearned.

6. In the parents I would fain have as much education as is possible. Nor do I refer to the fathers only. It is recorded that Cornelia, the mother of the Gracchi, contributed in no small degree to the eloquence of her sons, and posterity may still enjoy her cultured way of speech in the letters which have survived. Laelia too, the daughter of Gaius Laelius, is said to have reproduced in her speaking the elegance of her father, and the speech delivered by Hortensia, the daughter of Quintus Hortensius, in the presence of the triumvirs is still read, not simply out of courtesy to her sex.

7. Those who have not themselves enjoyed the benefits of education must not devote less care to the proper instruction of their children, and their own deficiencies (in learning) should make them the more careful in all other particulars.

Of the slave companions amongst whom the object of these high hopes is to be reared, the same may be said as of the nurses.

8. In the case of *paedagogi* (attendants) this further point should be insisted upon, that they be either thoroughly educated—and this I should like to be the first consideration—or else aware of their lack of education. Nothing is worse than those who have made some little progress beyond the first elements and on the strength of this are filled with a false idea of their own knowledge. For they are loth to surrender the role of teacher, and, as if by a legal right inherent in the power entrusted to them, whereby this type of man is usually puffed up, in dictatorial and often savage fashion they impart their own folly to their charges.

9. Their deficiencies too often harm the morals of the young. Thus Leonides, the *paedagogus* of Alexander the Great, according to Diogenes of Babylon, implanted in his youthful master certain vices which from that early training remained with him even when he was mature and already a great king.

10. If any one thinks that I am demanding a great deal, let him consider that it is an orator that is being trained: a difficult task even when nothing has failed us in moulding him; and further that other greater difficulties remain: for he must also have unceasing application, teachers of outstanding merit, and a wide range of studies.

11. And so the best principles must be laid down: if they prove irksome to any one, their failure lies with the man and not with the system of instruction. However, if our future orator is not so fortunate as to have such nurses, companions, and attendants as I should

most like him to have, at any rate let there be some one person constantly by his side, some one not unskilled in speaking, to correct at once any blunders in speech made by these others in the presence of his charge and so to prevent such blunders from taking root in his mind. Provided always it be understood that my former recommendations indicate the sound plan, and that this is only a palliative.

12. I prefer that a boy should start with the Greek language: first because he will pick up Latin, which is in common use, whether we wish it or no, and second because he should be instructed first in Greek studies from which ours derive their origin.

13. Yet I would not have such slavish adherence to this principle as to compel the boy to speak and study Greek only, for a considerable time, as is usually the custom. For in this way arise countless faults of pronunciation, through the corrupting influence of foreign sounds and faults of speech also to which Greek forms of expression cling through constant familiarity, persisting tenaciously even in the speaking of a different language.

14. Latin therefore should follow at no great interval and before long the two languages should advance together. Thus it will come to pass that when we begin to give equal attention to both languages neither one will hurt the other.

15. Some have thought that children under seven years of age should not be taught letters because that is the earliest age at which such studies can be understood and such toil endured. Until the time of Aristophanes the grammarian, it was a common tradition that Hesiod held this view. Aristophanes was the first

to deny to that poet the *Hypothekai* (Suggestions) in which this view is found.

16. But other writers too, including Eratosthenes, have preached the same doctrine. A better view is that held by those who like Chrysippus would have some instruction for every stage of the child's life. Chrysippus, though assigning the first three years to nurses, lays it down that even they should mould the child's mind by the best training possible.

17. But why should an age which is already dealing with morals have no dealings with letters? I am well aware that, in the whole space of time of which I am speaking, scarcely as much is achieved as can be bestowed by a single year when the child is older, yet it seems to me that our opponents have here spared the teacher rather than the pupil.

18. How will they be better employed, in any case, from the time when they can speak? For they must do something. Or why should we despise this gain, however small it may be, in the period prior to the seventh year? Assuredly, no matter how small the contribution of those earlier years, yet the child will learn greater things in that year which would otherwise have been devoted to the lesser.

19. And this gain, carried forward through the years, adds to the total, and time thus saved in infancy is an acquisition to youth.

Let the same rule be laid down for the years that follow so that the pupil may not be late in beginning to learn what every one has to learn. Let us not then lose the earliest years—the less so since the rudiments of letters depend on memory alone: and memory not only exists in small children but is also most tenacious at that stage.

20. Nor am I so ignorant of the capacities of different ages as to think that we should straightway place a grievous burden upon tender minds and remorselessly exact close application. For one thing especially must be guarded against, viz. lest one who cannot yet love studies come to hate them and even after the passing of childhood's years shrink from a bitter task once undergone.

Let this first instruction be in the form of play; let the pupil be asked questions and praised for his answers, let him never rejoice in ignorance of anything: sometimes, when he will not learn, let another be taught of whom he may be jealous: let him compete sometimes with others and quite often think himself victorious: let him also be excited by rewards, which at that age are eagerly sought after.

21. These are trivial matters we are expounding, we who profess to have the training of an orator. But even studies have their infancy and as the rearing of bodies, destined ere long to be of the stoutest, starts with milk and the cradle, so he who was to be the most eloquent of men once uttered an infant's wail and made the first attempts at speech with halting tongue and found difficulty in distinguishing the forms of the letters. And whilst a knowledge of certain things is not sufficient in itself, it is not therefore unnecessary to possess it.

22. But, if no one blames a father who considers these things worthy of attention in his own son's case, why should one be blamed for bringing to public notice things he would be right in doing in the privacy of his own home? It is the more necessary to do so, since younger minds take in smaller things more readily and as human bodies cannot be moulded to certain flexions

of the limbs save when they are tender, so with men's minds, strength itself when it comes makes them more unyielding in most respects.

23. Would Philip King of Macedon have chosen that the first rudiments of letters should be imparted to his son Alexander by Aristotle the greatest philosopher of the day, or would the latter have undertaken the task, save in the belief that the first elements in our studies are best handled by the best teachers and that these elements have an important bearing on the final result?

24. Let us pretend then that it is Alexander who is committed to our charge, placed on my lap, a child worthy of infinite care (though every man thinks that of his own child). Am I then to be ashamed to point out even in the very rudiments of instruction certain short-cuts to the end in view?

For example, I certainly do not approve of what I see to be common practice, viz. that children should learn the names and order of the letters before their forms.

25. This (practice) hinders the recognition of the letters since the child soon ceases to attend to their shapes and simply follows his memory which outstrips his observation. And so teachers even when they seem to have fixed the letters firmly enough in the minds of their pupils in the straightforward order in which they are at first usually written, hark back again and by varying the arrangement introduce confusion until their pupils know the letters by their appearance and not by their sequence. Thus, as in the case of persons, so in the case of letters they will best be taught appearance and name together.

26. But what is a hindrance in the case of letters will do no harm with syllables.

Further, I approve of a practice devised to stimulate

the child to learn, viz. that of giving him ivory letters to play with and anything else that can be proved to add to the child's pleasure, which it may be a delight to him to handle, look at, and name.

27. When the child begins to trace the outlines of the letters it will be useful to have them cut out on a board, in as beautiful a script as possible, so that his pen may be guided along them as if in furrows. Thus he will not go wrong as in writing on waxen tablets (for he will be confined within the edges on either side and will therefore be unable to deviate from his model), and by tracing definite outlines with greater speed and frequency he will develop the proper muscles and will not require the helping hand of a teacher placed upon his own.

28. Important, too, in this connexion is a matter which is often apt to be neglected by educated people, I mean care in writing neatly and quickly. For since writing itself is the most essential thing in our studies and the one thing from which alone springs true and deeply rooted proficiency, a slow pen hinders thought and a badly formed and slovenly hand cannot be deciphered. This involves the labour of dictating what has to be written over again.

29. Wherefore always and everywhere, but especially in private and familiar letters, it will be a source of pleasure to have given attention even to this small matter.

30. There is no short cut to the learning of syllables. They must all be learnt by heart; nor, as is frequently the case, should the more difficult be postponed till they are dealt with in writing words.

31. Nay, more—we must not even trust unduly to a first learning by heart. It will be found more profitable

to go back and spend much time in driving them home, and in reading, too, not to hurry on to continuous or quick reading until a clear and unhesitating joining of the letters has been attained without at any rate any pausing for thought. Then with these syllables let words be formed and so let the pupil begin to weave sentences together.

32. It is incredible how reading is retarded by undue haste. This gives rise to hesitation, stumbling, and repetition on the part of pupils who venture beyond their powers, and then when they go astray, lack confidence even in what they already know.

33. Let reading, then, be first of all confident, then connected, and for a long time let it be slow till by practice correctness and speed are achieved together.

34. For to keep looking to the right, as is always taught, and to see ahead are matters not only of theory but also of practice, since the reader has to pronounce what comes first while he looks at what follows, and most difficult of all, the attention of the mind has to be divided so that one thing is done with the voice, another with the eyes.

When the child begins to write words in the ordinary course it will be worth while to see that he does not waste his labour on common words chosen haphazard.

35. For whilst engaged on something else, he will from the very first be able to learn the meaning of more recondite terms to which the Greeks give the name γλῶσσαι, and on the threshold of his studies to master something which otherwise will demand its own special time for study.

Since we are still dwelling on matters of slight importance, I would urge that lines set as models for copying should not convey idle sentiments but some useful instruction.

36. Recollections of such maxims remain with a man till he is old and when impressed upon a mind still unformed will even aid in building character. The sayings of famous men, too, and chosen passages, especially from the poets (for the youthful mind finds greater pleasure in learning poetry), may be learnt by heart as a relaxation. A good memory is a prime essential in oratory, as I shall explain in due course, and memory is best strengthened and nourished by exercise. Moreover, in those years of which we are now speaking, still incapable of producing anything original, memory is practically the only mental power which can profit by a teacher's care.

37. To give freedom of speech and clearness of pronunciation it will be found useful to demand from pupils of this age that they roll forth as quickly as possible words and lines of studied difficulty, made up of a series of clashing syllables and as it were broken in sound: in Greek these are called χαλινοί (bridles or bits). Such practice is a trifling thing to speak of, but if it be neglected, many faults of speech not removed in early years remain for life through force of evil habit, which cannot afterwards be corrected.

CHAPTER 2

THE COMPARATIVE MERITS OF PRIVATE AND PUBLIC INSTRUCTION

1. But now let our young pupil begin gradually to grow and to leave his mother's lap and begin serious studies. The most important question now is whether it is better to keep the student in the privacy of his own home or to hand him over to a large school and to what may be termed public instructors.

2. The latter course, I observe, has won the approval not only of those who have moulded the manners of most famous states but also of the most eminent authorities on education. It must, however, be admitted that some disagree with this wellnigh universal practice on grounds of private opinion. Two considerations in particular appear to weigh with these critics. The first is that it is safer on moral grounds to avoid a throng of youths whose age is peculiarly prone to vicious practices, whence it is claimed—and I would the claim were false—that evil consequences have frequently arisen.

The second consideration is this, that no matter who the future teacher is, it seems likely that if he has but one pupil he will devote his time more freely to him than if he has to share that time amongst several.

3. The former plea is by far the more important. For if it were admitted that schools, whilst affording better instruction, do harm to morals, I should judge the principles of right living of more importance than those of the noblest oratory. But to my mind the two things are inseparably bound up together.

For I hold that a man cannot be a true orator without

being a good man too, nor do I wish to see the two dissociated even if it be possible.

I shall therefore deal with this point before taking up the other.

4. It is thought that in schools morals are corrupted. Now it is perfectly true that this does happen sometimes, but it happens in the home also: and of that we have countless instances, just as we have countless instances of the maintenance in both places of a spotless reputation. It is the natural disposition of the boy and the care taken of him which make all the difference. Given a mind inclined towards things evil, given carelessness in the moulding and guarding of the boy's purity in early years, and it will be found that seclusion offers just as good an opportunity for evil practices. For a private tutor may be a scoundrel, and intercourse with wicked slaves is no safer than intercourse with immoral youths of free birth.

5. But if the boy's natural disposition is good and if the parents are not sunk in blind and careless sloth, it is possible to choose the noblest instructors (and that is the foremost consideration with wise parents) and a system of instruction of the strictest kind, and at the same time to place at the boy's side some friend of weighty character or some faithful freedman whose constant companionship may even reclaim those of whom the parents were afraid.

6. It were an easy task to demolish fears on that score. Would that we did not ourselves corrupt the morals of our children! Even in earliest infancy we spoil them by our indulgence. The soft way in which we bring them up, calling it kindness, saps all strength of mind and body. What will the child not covet when

he is a grown man, if he creeps about in purple? Before he is pronouncing his first words, he knows what 'cook' means and cries for oysters. We train their palates before we train their speech.

7. They grow up lolling in litters and if they ever touch the ground, it is clinging to supporting hands on either side. We take delight in their naughty sayings: words that would not be tolerated even in our pet boys from Alexandria we hail with laughter and kisses.

Nor is it strange that our children should utter such words, for we teach them ourselves, they hear them from us.

8. They see our courtesans, and our boy favourites. Every banquet makes lewd songs re-echo through the house. Shameful sights are revealed to our children's eyes. Thus is bred familiarity, till such things become quite natural. The poor victims learn these vicious lessons ere they know them to be vicious, and then, dissolute and weak, instead of picking up these evil things at school, they take them thither with them.

9. But, it will be urged, in the matter of studies a single teacher will have more time to give, if he has but a single pupil. Now, in the first place there is nothing to hinder this single private pupil, whoever he may be, from being identical with the pupil taught at school.

But even if it were impossible to combine public and private instruction, I should have preferred the light of an honourable assembly to the darkness of solitude. For all the best teachers delight in crowded class-rooms and consider themselves worthy of a still larger audience.

10. But less able teachers as a rule, from a conscious-

ness of their own failings, are content to stick to single pupils and to perform what is in a way the duty of a *paedagogus* (attendant).

11. Supposing, however, that through power or wealth or friendship a parent can secure a splendid, nay an unrivalled, teacher to instruct his son in his own home, still that teacher is not going to spend the whole day upon one pupil. Can the attention of any pupil be so continuously on the stretch, without growing weary, as the eyes do by constant gazing at a single object? And there is this special consideration, that study calls for far more solitary application than actual instruction.

12. The teacher does not stand beside the pupil when he is writing or learning things by heart or thinking—indeed, when one is doing any of these things any one's interposition is a hindrance. Reading, too, does not in every case and all the time require guidance or interpretation. For when could one become acquainted with the countless authors to be studied? The time devoted to instruction, then, is but a small fraction in which the work is marshalled, so to speak, for the whole day.

13. Accordingly instruction can be given to several pupils in succession even in cases where individual attention is required.

But much instruction can be conveyed by the voice of one teacher to all his pupils simultaneously. I say nothing of the analyses and declamations of the rhetoricians, for however great the audience each individual hearer will carry off the whole thing with him.

14. The voice of the teacher, then, is not like a banquet where there is less for each in proportion as more partake of it, but rather resembles the sun shedding

upon all alike the same amount of light and heat. So, too, if a professor of literature expounds the principles of speaking or unravels knotty points of interpretation, explains historical problems or interprets poetry, all his audience will be instructed at one and the same time.

15. But, it will be said, for correction and for preparation numbers are a hindrance. Suppose that is true (is there anything at all that gives absolute satisfaction?), we shall in a moment weigh that disadvantage against the advantages of public instruction. Some one else will urge, 'Yes, but I do not wish a boy to be sent to a place where he will be neglected.' Now, you will find that a good teacher does not burden himself with a greater number of pupils than he can manage. Further, we must be careful above all things else to secure the intimate friendship of such a master, so that in teaching he may not simply be guided by a sense of duty, but also by affection for his pupil. In this way we shall never be mere units in a throng.

16. Again, no master who has the slightest tinge of culture will fail to give special encouragement, for his own glory's sake as well as for his pupil's, to any one in whom he discovers application and aptitude.

Supposing, then, that large schools are to be avoided (and even that I do not admit, in cases where a teacher is popular by reason of his excellence), still that does not mean that all schools are to be shunned. For it is one thing to avoid them, another to choose amongst them.

17. And now, if I have demolished the objections to public instruction, I shall proceed to state my own views on the matter.

18. First and foremost, let the future orator, whose

life is to be spent in great assemblies and in the blaze of public life, become accustomed from his earliest years to face men unabashed and not grow pale by living in solitude and so to say in the cloister's shade. The mind requires constant stimulus and excitement, but in such retirement it either flags and rusts as it were in the gloom or else becomes swollen with empty self-conceit. For one who does not match himself with others must needs overrate his own powers.

19. Then when he must display the fruits of his study, he gropes about in broad daylight and finds everything new and strange, as is natural with one who has learnt in solitude what has to be done amidst a throng.

20. I pass over the friendships formed at school. They last in undiminished strength through life, and are sealed with a kind of religious sanction. For to be initiated into the same studies is as sacred a bond as to be initiated into the same mysteries of religion.

Where will our pupil pick up what is known as 'common sense', if he has avoided society? For the gregarious instinct belongs not merely to human beings but even to dumb animals.

21. Further, at home he can only learn what he himself is taught, but at school what is taught to others also. Every day he will hear many things approved, many things corrected; he will profit by another's sloth rebuked, another's industry commended. Words of praise will stir him to emulation.

22. He will think it disgraceful to be surpassed by pupils of his age, and a fine thing to have beaten his seniors. All these things stimulate the mind, and though ambition may in itself be a vice, none the less it is frequently the source of virtues.

23. There is one useful method known to me, which was employed by my own teachers. They arranged us in classes, determining the order of speaking according to the ability of the pupils. Thus as each boy appeared to excel in proficiency he stood higher in the order of declamation.

24. Tests of progress were held from time to time, and to earn promotion was a great prize with us, whilst to be head of the class was by far the most coveted honour.

The class order was not decided once for all. Each month gave the vanquished a fresh opportunity to do battle. Thus those who held high places through previous success did not relax their efforts, and shame stirred the less successful to strive to wipe out their disgrace.

25. So far as I can form a conjecture, I would maintain that this rivalry did far more to kindle our zeal for oratorical studies than the exhortations of teachers, the care of *paedagogi* (attendants), and the wishes of our parents.

26. Amongst more advanced students of literature, then, rivalry stimulates progress. In the case of beginners and those whose minds are still unformed, imitation of their fellow pupils is more pleasant than attempts to imitate the master, for the reason that it is easier. Those who are learning the rudiments will scarcely dare aspire to hopes of achieving what they look upon as the very highest eloquence. They will rather fasten upon what is nearer to them, just as vines twining round trees, cling first to the lower branches before they reach the tops.

27. So true is this principle that even the master

himself (if indeed he will set usefulness before vain-glory) must make it his business, in dealing with minds still unformed, not to start by overloading the feeble intellects of his pupils, but to control his own powers and come down to the level of their understanding.

28. For just as narrow-necked jars spill a flood of liquid poured over them, whereas they fill up when it flows in gradually or even drop by drop, so we must observe carefully the capacity of youthful minds. For that which is too difficult for their understanding will not find entrance to the boys' minds which, if we may put it so, have too narrow an opening for its reception.

29. It is useful, then, for the pupil to have those whom he may seek first to imitate, then to surpass. In this way hopes of yet higher achievement will gradually be formed.

There is this further consideration, that teachers themselves cannot in the presence of single pupils feel the same mental stimulus and exhilaration in speaking as they do when inspired by the large audiences a school affords.

30. The most important factor in eloquence is a certain state of mind. The orator's mind must be roused, it must form images of objects and, in a sense, be transformed into the nature of the things of which he speaks. Further, the nobler and the loftier the mind of the orator, the more powerful the springs, if I may say so, of its action. And so it feeds upon applause, it expands in its whirling flight, it glories in the consciousness of great achievement.

31. On the other hand, the orator feels a kind of silent disdain in lowering to the instruction of a single pupil the noble power of eloquence won by such mighty

labour. He feels ashamed to rise above the level of ordinary conversation. And, indeed, let any one imagine the style of one declaiming, or the voice, gesture, and pronunciation of a pleader, the animation in short of both mind and body, the effort, to speak of nothing else, and the fatigue involved—all before an audience of one! Would such an orator not seem to be affected with something very like madness? There would be no such thing as eloquence amongst men, if we only spoke with one man at a time.

CHAPTER 3

METHODS OF DISCERNING ABILITY IN THE YOUNG AND OF HANDLING THEM

1. THE skilled teacher, when a pupil is entrusted to his care, will first of all seek to discover his ability and natural disposition. A good memory is the chief indication of ability in a pupil and its excellence lies in two things, ease in acquiring knowledge and accuracy in retaining it. Next comes the faculty of imitation, for that also is characteristic of a teachable nature, i.e. provided that the pupil reproduces what he is taught and not a person's appearance, for example, and gait and any unfortunate peculiarity he may have.

2. The pupil who seeks to rouse laughter by his excellence in imitation of this sort, will not afford me any hope of outstanding ability. For from the very beginning the truly talented boy will also be well behaved; if it were otherwise I should have held that it is just as well to be dull in intellect as to be clever and ill mannered. But the well-behaved will be far different from such slothful and idle fellows.

3. My ideal pupil will readily acquire the knowledge presented to him and some things, too, he will elicit by questions: yet he will follow his master rather than seek to outrun him. Such precocity of intellect seldom, if ever, attains to full fruition.

4. These are the boys who dispatch trifling tasks with ease and, carried away by self-confidence, straightway make a show of such attainments. But their attainments are entirely superficial: they string words together and display their facility unabashed and un-

hampered by any tinge of modesty. Their performances have glibness but no depth;

5. and there is no true strength underlying them, deep and firmly rooted. Even as seeds scattered on the surface spring up too quickly, and grasses, feigning the promise of the young green corn, grow yellow with empty ears before the harvest. The performance of such youthful prodigies gives pleasure when one considers their years: then their progress ceases and our admiration wanes.

6. When the teacher has noticed the points I have mentioned, let him next observe how the mind of his pupil is to be handled. Some boys are lazy unless you urge them on, some do not brook commands, some are restrained by fear, some dispirited by it, some are fashioned by long-continued application, some make greater progress through spurts of hard work. Mine be the pupil who kindles at a word of praise, who glories in distinction, who weeps at defeat.

7. He must be nourished with hopes of success, he will feel the sting of reproof, desire for glory will spur him on: in such a pupil I shall never be afraid of idleness.

8. Some relaxation, however, must be given to all, not only because there is no single thing which can endure unceasing toil, and even inanimate and lifeless objects, to be able to preserve their energy, relax as it were in alternating periods of rest, but also because zeal for learning depends upon inclination, a thing which cannot be forced.

9. Thus pupils refreshed and restored by recreation bring more energy to their studies and a keener mind, whereas the mind as a rule refuses tasks imposed by harsh compulsion.

10. Nor should I be displeased by love of play in my pupils (for this, too, is a sign of keenness), nor could I hope that a pupil who is always sombre and downcast would show alertness of mind in his studies, seeing that he would fail in the impetuosity which is also most natural at such an age.

11. Only let there be moderation in their recreations, so that on the one hand refusal to allow them may not breed hatred of studies, and on the other indulgence to excess may not foster the love of idleness. Some games, too, are useful for sharpening the pupils' wits, e.g. when they compete with each other in asking questions of all sorts in turn.

12. True character, too, reveals itself with less reserve in play: and let us remember that no child is so tender in years as not to learn at once the distinction between right and wrong, and that he requires to be moulded with the greatest care at the age when he is still innocent of deceit and yields most readily to his instructors. For you would sooner break than bend straight those who have once become set in vicious habits.

13. From the beginning, then, the boy must be exhorted never to show selfishness or dishonesty or lack of self-control, and Virgil's precept is ever to be kept in mind: 'So powerful are habits formed in tender age.'

14. As for corporal punishment, though it is a recognized practice and though Chrysippus does not object to it, I am altogether opposed to it, first because it is disgusting, fit only for slaves and undoubtedly an insult (as appears, if you change the age of the victim): in the next place, because a pupil whose mind so ill befits a free man's son as not to be corrected by reproof, will

remain obdurate even in face of blows—like the vilest of slaves: and finally because such chastisement will be quite unnecessary if there is some one ever present to supervise the boy's studies with diligence.

15. As things are, it seems usually to happen that the carelessness of *paedagogi* is amended by the pupils being punished for doing what is wrong instead of being compelled to do what is right.

Then again, if you coerce the young child by means of blows, how would you deal with the grown youth who cannot thus be driven by fear and has more important things to learn?

16. Remember too that, when children are beaten, many unseemly cries, of which they will afterwards be ashamed, often escape them in their grief or fear, and the shame of this breaks and humiliates the spirit and makes them, sick at heart, shun the very light of day.

17. Now if, in choosing guardians and teachers, too little care has been taken to select those of sterling moral character, I am ashamed to mention the shameful practices for which men make this right of corporal punishment an excuse, and the opportunity sometimes afforded to others too by the terror of it in the wretched child's mind. I shall not dwell upon this topic: what is understood (by the reader) is already more than enough. Suffice it to say this: no one ought to have undue liberty in dealing with an age that is still feeble and helpless in face of ill treatment.

18. I shall now begin to speak of the branches of study necessary in the training of a pupil who is to be moulded into a potential orator, and explain which of them should be begun at the different stages in his education.

CHAPTER 4

GRAMMAR

1. WHEN a boy has learned to read and write with ease, he must come first of all under the care of the grammarians. It matters not whether I speak of the Greek or of the Latin grammarian, though I prefer the Greek to have precedence; but both pursue the same method.

2. The range of instruction which these teachers profess to cover may be divided very briefly into two parts, the art of speaking correctly (i.e. grammar in the modern sense) and the interpretation of the poets. But within its recesses the subject includes more than appears on the surface.

3. For with speaking is also joined the theory of writing, and the interpretation of the poets is preceded by correct reading, whilst the art of criticism is associated with both. Indeed the old grammarians employed that art in the most drastic fashion. Not only did they make free to mark lines with the stigma of a censor, so to speak, and to remove as changelings from an author's family books which in their opinion had been falsely ascribed to him, but they also formed a canon to which they admitted some authors while excluding others.

4. Further, it is not enough to have read the poets: all manner of writings must be ransacked not only for the subject-matter but also for words, which often gain their authority from the writers who use them. Then again grammar cannot be complete without a study of music, since it has to pronounce on questions of metre and rhythm; nor could it make the poets intelligible

without a knowledge of astronomy, for, to take a single instance, in indicating the seasons of the year they constantly refer to the rising and setting of constellations. Again a knowledge of philosophy is essential to grammar, not only because of the countless passages in almost every poem derived from the most intimate and subtle mysteries of natural science, but also for the sake of Empedocles in Greek, and Varro and Lucretius in Latin, literature: writers who have embodied the teaching of philosophy in their verse.

5. And yet again there is need of no slight eloquence to enable grammar to pronounce with accuracy and fluency upon the various subjects I have mentioned.

For these reasons we have no sympathy with critics who decry the study of grammar on the ground that it is trivial and dry. Unless the foundations of the future orator have been well and truly laid by this study, all the learning you build upon them will fall to the ground. It is a branch of knowledge which is necessary in youth and pleasant in old age, a sweet companion in retirement, the only one in the whole range of studies which has in it more usefulness than empty show.

6. Let no one then despise the elements of grammar as trivial things, not because it is a difficult task to distinguish consonants from vowels and to subdivide them into semi-vowels and mutes, but because those who enter the inner shrine, as it were, of this sanctuary will come into the presence of many mysteries fitted not merely to sharpen the wits of boys but to give scope for the exercise of the profoundest erudition and knowledge.

[*The passage which follows, Chapter* 4. 7 *to Chapter* 7. 29, *is omitted as being less important to the student of the history of Education than to the specialist in the study of the Latin language; to the latter it is a mine of valuable information. Quintilian explains and illustrates copiously from Latin the minutiae of grammar with which the grammarian must deal, including in his treatment the following topics:*

The parts of speech; barbarisms and solecisms; accentuation; figures of speech; the bases of language, analogy, authority, custom; etymology; orthography; differences between spelling and pronunciation.

We resume at Chapter 7. 30.]

CHAPTER 7

GRAMMAR (*cont.*)

30. But in all these questions let the grammarian exercise his own judgement: for his criticism should carry great weight. My own view (on the question of spelling and pronunciation) is that except in cases where usage is firmly established, every word should be written as it is pronounced.

31. For the function of letters is to preserve our utterances and to convey to readers what has been entrusted to letters for safe keeping. Thus they ought to express exactly what we intend to say.

32. These are the main topics which concern correctness in spelling and in writing: the two remaining subjects, viz. appositeness and elegance in speaking, I do not seek to take away from the grammarians but, since I have still to speak of the duties of the teacher of rhetoric, I reserve them for treatment in a more important part of my work.

33. But there recurs to me the thought that there will be critics who think that the topics that I have mentioned are too trivial and only serve to encumber those who are concerned with something more important. Nor do I myself believe that we ought to descend to mere hair-splitting and foolish quibbling, and I agree that the minds of pupils are blunted and weakened by such pedantry.

34. But no part of grammar is harmful save what is superfluous. Or was Marcus Tullius less of an orator because he also devoted much attention to this branch of study and, as appears from his letters, sternly exacted

correctness of speech from his son? Or did the publication of his books on 'Analogy' weaken the intellectual vigour of Gaius Caesar?

35. Or was Messala less eloquent a speaker because he devoted whole books not merely to single words but even to single letters? Grammatical studies are harmful not to those who pass through them but to those who never get beyond them.

CHAPTER 8

GRAMMAR (*cont.*)

1. It remains to deal with Reading. To instruct a pupil in this subject as to where he should check his breathing, where he should mark the pause in a line, where the sense of a sentence is completed and where it begins, when the voice should be raised or lowered, how the voice should be modulated in each case and what is the requisite degree of slowness or of speed, of animation or of gentleness—all these are things which can only be demonstrated to pupils in actual practice.

2. There is, therefore, only one general principle which I would lay down here to enable my pupil to do all these things correctly, viz. let him *understand* what he is reading. Moreover, his reading should be above all things manly and dignified, with a certain degree of sweetness: not indeed like the reading of prose, because it is poetry he is reading and the poets themselves bear witness that they are singers, yet not degraded to a careless sing-song or to that effeminate and affected drawl which is the fashion nowadays, a mannerism most fittingly rebuked, as we read, by Gaius Caesar while he was still a boy, in these words: 'If you are singing, you are singing badly; and if you are reading, you are singing.'

3. Further, I would not have my pupil indulge in impersonations after the manner of the comic stage, as some teachers advocate, yet I do wish that there should be a certain modulation of the voice, whereby such passages may be distinguished from those in which the poet speaks in his own person.

4. In general, much careful training is required to secure above all things else that tender minds, which will retain a deep impression of whatever is presented to them when they are still unformed and ignorant, may learn not merely what is eloquent, but far rather what is morally good.

5. And therefore it is an eminently sound practice to begin reading with Homer and Virgil, though maturer judgement is required for a full understanding of their merits. But for that there is time enough, for they will be read more than once. Meanwhile, let the pupil's mind soar to the sublime levels of epic song, and draw the breath of inspiration from the majesty of its theme and become imbued with its noble sentiments.

6. Tragedies are useful and the lyric poets nourish the youthful mind provided always that you select not only suitable authors but also suitable passages from their works. For there is much loose morality among the Greek lyrists, nor would I choose to expound Horace in certain passages.

Elegies, at any rate those on erotic themes, and poems in hendecasyllabics, the short metre of Sotadean verse (a type of poetry which a teacher should never even mention) should be kept out of the course of reading if possible or, if not, they should be reserved for an age of greater strength and maturity.

7. Comedy may contribute in a most useful way to eloquence, for it runs through the whole gamut of character and emotion, but of its use in the education of our pupils I shall speak a little later in the proper place. When once their moral character is firmly established it will deserve a prominent place in their studies. I speak of Menander, but I do not exclude other writers of comedy.

8. Latin authors, too, will make their due contribution, but boys must first read what is best calculated to nourish talent and stimulate mental development. For other studies, which pertain to learning simply, the long years of life will afford an ample field. But the old Latin writers also are most valuable, though most of them were stronger in natural genius than in artistry: especially do they give us a wealth of language, while their dignity appears in their tragedies, their eloquence, and what may be styled Attic charm in their comedies.

9. In them, too, will be found more careful arrangement than in most of the moderns, who have taken the view that the sole merit of their work lies in the thoughts they express. And certainly it is to the ancients that we must look for austere integrity and what I may call manly strength, for we moderns have descended to all manner of effeminate and vicious refinement in our theory of eloquence as in other things.

10. Finally let us follow the lead of the noblest orators, who employ the ancient poets to strengthen a case or to adorn their eloquence (to point a moral or adorn a tale).

11. Especially in Cicero, but frequently too in Asinius and the others who most nearly approach these two masters, we see verses quoted from Ennius, Accius, Pacuvius, Lucilius, Terentius, Caecilius and others, verses which are most effective not only in displaying the erudition of the speaker, but also in giving pleasure to the hearer whose ears are soothed amid the harsh din of the law courts with the pleasant cadences of poetry.

12. Such quotations serve another most useful

purpose, for the orators confirm their arguments by the utterances of the poets as by so many pieces of further evidence. But my former observations on the value of such studies have more particular reference to boys; the latter refer to men of more mature age, since the love of grammar and the advantages of reading are not confined to school days but last throughout a man's whole life.

13. In lecturing, the grammarian will also have to give attention to minor matters, e.g. he should require that a line of poetry be analysed and the different parts of speech named to him, and again he should deal with the peculiarities of the different metrical feet which must be known in connexion with poetry, and are also required in oratorical prose.

14. He must detect barbarous and inappropriate expressions and contraventions of the laws of speech. His purpose will not be to blame the poets in these respects at any rate, for since they are for the most part compelled to obey the rules of metre they are treated with such indulgence that these very faults are called by other names in the case of poetry; thus we speak of metaplasms (irregularities in declension) and 'schemata' (poetical figures) as I have said, and, making a virtue of their necessity, accord them our approval. The purpose then of the grammarian in drawing attention to these points will rather be to instruct his pupils in the devices of the poetic art and to exercise their memories.

15. It is also useful in dealing with elementary instruction to point out the various meanings which individual words may bear. And not the least part of the teacher's care will be devoted to 'glossemata', words

of rare occurrence (or foreign origin) which require explanation.

16. But far more care must be taken in teaching all the tropes, which are the especial ornaments not only of a poem but also of an oration, and both types of 'schemata', those styled figures of speech and those styled figures of thought. The treatment of these and also the tropes I postpone till I shall have occasion to speak of the adornment of an oration.

17. Above all else let the teacher impress upon his pupils the value of skilful arrangement, and of appropriateness in the treatment of a subject, what is best suited to each type of character, what is praiseworthy in feeling and in language, where diffuseness and where restraint are to be commended.

18. The work of the grammarian will also include the interpretation of allusions in the poets, a task which calls indeed for care but not for superfluous labour. It is sufficient to have expounded the received interpretation or at most those mentioned by authors of repute. To ferret out all that has been said even by the most contemptible authorities is too irksome to be worth while or else it is merely a parade of empty erudition and hinders and blunts intelligences that were better freed for other things.

19. He who searches through every scrap of writing that bears on a point, even what is not worth reading, is just the man to waste his labour on old wives' tales. And the commentaries of the grammarians are full of such rubbish, while even the authors of these books themselves are not very familiar with their contents.

20. It is a well-known fact that Didymus, the most voluminous writer who ever lived, objected on one

occasion to some story as being false and was then confronted with a book of his own which contained the very story in question.

21. And this happens in the case of imaginary tales to a ridiculous, sometimes to a shameful, extent and unscrupulous writers enjoy the greatest freedom in concocting most of their materials. They invent whole books and authors, as it occurs to them, in perfect safety, because authors who never existed cannot be produced in evidence against them: whereas, in dealing with the better known authors, they are often convicted of inaccuracy by careful readers.

Accordingly I shall account it a merit in a grammarian to confess to a certain degree of ignorance.

CHAPTER 9

THE DUTIES OF A GRAMMARIAN

1. I HAVE now dealt with two portions of the instruction which the teacher of grammar professes to impart, viz. the theory of speaking and the interpretation of authors: these are styled respectively 'method' and 'interpretation'.

2. Let us add, however, to the curriculum certain elements in the art of speaking in which he may train pupils not yet old enough to go to the school of rhetoric.

They should learn then to recite, in pure and unaffected diction, fables such as those of Aesop, which come immediately after the stories of their nurses, and then to achieve the same gracefulness in writing them. First they must learn to break up lines of poetry, then to put the meaning into other words, and then to paraphrase more boldly, with freedom to curtail or to adorn provided only that the meaning of the poet remains unchanged.

3. Such paraphrasing is not an easy task even for accomplished teachers and one who has handled it in an adequate fashion will be fit to learn anything.

In the grammarian's school, too, the pupil must learn to note *maxims* and *topics for discussion* and *character-sketches*, with an account added of the meanings of the sentences noted. For these arise naturally out of his reading. The principle in all these exercises is the same but the form varies, for the maxim is of universal application whereas the character-sketch is limited to the persons concerned.

4. There are several types of 'topics', according to

the usual account of them. One resembles the maxim, taking the form of a simple statement 'He said' or 'He used to say'. Another takes the form of a reply, 'In answer to a question he said' or 'When this was said to him, he replied'. A third is not unlike this, 'When some one had said or done something'.

5. Even in men's actions it is held that topics may be found, e.g. 'When Crates saw an ignorant boy, he smote his master'. There is also another form very like this, though the grammarians do not venture to give it the same name but simply call it 'topical in kind', e.g. 'When Milo had practised carrying a calf, he carried it after it had grown to be a bull'.

In all these exercises the pupil must go through the declension of the same cases and he must give an account both of the actions involved and of the words spoken.

6. Short stories rendered famous by the poets should also be handled, not, in my opinion, for the purpose of eloquence but for general information. There are other matters involving greater labour and more energy which the Latin teachers of rhetoric have neglected and so made a necessary part of the grammarian's curriculum. The Greeks have realized more adequately the weight and measure of their duties (as teachers of rhetoric).

CHAPTER 10

IS A KNOWLEDGE OF A VARIETY OF SUBJECTS NECESSARY FOR THE FUTURE ORATOR?

1. I have now dealt as briefly as possible with the subject of Grammar, my purpose being not to say everything about it—an infinite task—but merely what is most necessary. Now I shall add a short survey of other branches of instruction in which I think pupils ought to be trained before they are handed over to the teacher of rhetoric, so that the circle of studies which the Greeks call ἐγκύκλιος παιδεία may be completed.

2. The study of other subjects, too, should be started in these early years; and as they are themselves separate arts and can be acquired in their completeness without a knowledge of the art of pleading, and since, moreover, they are not in themselves sufficient to make an orator, the question arises whether it is necessary to speak of them in the present work.

3. For, say some, what use is it to a man in conducting a case or in giving expert legal opinion to know how equilateral triangles can be constructed upon a given straight line? Or how will a man be a better advocate or counsellor if he has learned to distinguish the notes of the lyre by their names and intervals?

4. And perhaps they may go on to enumerate many orators who have been ever so effective in the courts and who never attended a lecture on geometry and knew musicians only through the pleasure enjoyed by every one in listening to their performances. To these critics I would first of all point out, what Marcus Cicero

frequently remarked in the book he wrote for Marcus Brutus, that we are not training such an orator as exists or has existed, but we have formed in our minds an ideal conception of the perfect orator who is not deficient in any respect whatsoever.

5. The philosophers, in fashioning the perfectly wise man, who is to be complete in every respect and, as they say, a god upon earth, not only maintain that he should be trained in a knowledge of all things divine or human, but also lead their pupil through a series of exercises which, considered in themselves, are certainly of trifling importance, being merely problems carefully devised for the stage to which the pupil has attained. Not because puzzles about horns or crocodiles can make a man wise, but because a perfectly wise man ought not to be at fault even in the most trifling questions.

6. In the same way, the teacher of geometry or of music, or any other subjects which I shall add to these, will not make an orator, who ought to be a wise man, but these studies, in addition to his own special studies, will help him towards perfection.

Let us take a parallel case. Antidotes to poisons and other compounds, such as salves which heal sore eyes or wounds, are, we observe, made up of a large number of ingredients, often contrary to each other in their effects, and out of these diverse elements is made the one mixture which is unlike any of its ingredients but takes its own peculiar properties from them all.

7. Or again, the voiceless insects from various kinds of flowers and juices make honey, the wondrous flavour of which no human cleverness can counterfeit. Shall we then be surprised if eloquence, the noblest gift of Providence to man, requires a wide range of studies

which, even if they do not display themselves in speech or show prominently, are none the less a source of hidden strength and reveal themselves despite their silence?

8. 'So-and-so was eloquent without these arts.'—Yes, but it is the perfect orator I seek to train.

'They don't help much.'—Still, it will not be a complete whole in the same way, if even minute portions are missing. And that perfection is such a complete whole will be admitted; and even if our hopes of attaining to it are in the highest degree precarious, still we ought to lay down all the means whereby they may be fulfilled, so that at any rate more may be achieved than would otherwise be the case. But why should we be faint-hearted? Nature does not forbid the existence of the perfect orator, and it is disgraceful to despair of anything that is possible.

Music

9. For myself I could be perfectly satisfied by the judgement of the ancients. Who does not know that Music, to speak of it first, even in those bygone days commanded not only so much attention but also so much veneration that the same men were adjudged musicians and prophets and philosophers, Orpheus and Linus, to take no other examples. According to the tradition of later times these two were both the sons of gods, and the former, because he soothed savage boorish hearts with a love for his music, was spoken of as having drawn not only the wild creatures but even rocks and forests in his train.

10. Similarly, too, Timagenes tells us that amongst all the humane studies Music stood out as the most

ancient, and most famous poets, too, bear witness, for in their writings the praises of heroes and of gods were sung at royal banquets to the music of the lute. Does not the great bard Iopas in Virgil sing of 'the wandering moon and the labours of the sun' and so forth? Assuredly the illustrious poet thus openly proclaims that music is linked with a knowledge even of things divine.

11. Now if that is granted, it will also be required for the training of the orator—if indeed, as we have said, that province as well which the orators abandoned and the philosophers seized upon, belonged really to us and if eloquence cannot be complete without a knowledge of all such things.

12. Yet no one has really doubted that men famous on account of their wisdom have been keen students of music. Pythagoras and his followers have rendered popular a view undoubtedly inherited by them from antiquity, viz. that the universe itself is constructed in accordance with a law which was afterwards imitated by the music of the lyre, and, not content with that concord of different elements to which the name 'harmony' is given, they gave a kind of music to the celestial motions.

13. In many passages and especially in the *Timaeus*, Plato can only be understood by those who have devoted careful study to this branch of learning, as well as to philosophy. I am speaking of philosophers—Socrates their fountain-head himself was not ashamed even in his old age to learn to play upon the lyre.

14. It is on record that great leaders have sung to the accompaniment of stringed instruments and flutes and that Spartan armies were kindled to battle by

strains of music. What other purpose have the horns and trumpets in our own Roman legions? Nay, in proportion to the surpassing loudness of their blended notes, so does the glory of the Romans in war surpass that of all other peoples.

15. It was not, then, without good reason that Plato believed music to be necessary for the true citizen, to whom he gave the name πολιτικός. Even the leaders of that philosophic sect which some regard as most austere, others as unduly harsh, were disposed to think that some philosophers would devote a certain amount of attention to these studies, and Lycurgus, author of the very sternest laws of the Spartans, approved of a training in music.

16. Nay, even Nature herself seems to have given us music as a gift to lighten the burden of toil: for songs cheer the sailor straining at the oar, and not only is music an aid to labour in those tasks in which the efforts of many are invited and controlled by the rhythmic measure of some pleasant voice, but even the weariness of solitary toil is soothed by melody, no matter how artless it may be.

17. So far I seem to be sounding the praises of the fairest of the arts without linking it up with the orator. Let us therefore pass over the further point that grammar and music were once closely associated. Indeed, Archytas and Evenus thought that grammar was subordinate to music. That the same men were teachers of both subjects is proved by Sophron, a writer of mimes to be sure, but one so much admired by Plato, that that philosopher is believed to have had his works under his head in his dying hour.

18. Eupolis bears like testimony, for in his plays

Prodamus is a teacher both of music and of letters, while Maricas, who in the play represents the demagogue Hyperbolus, confesses that he knows nothing of music except the letters of the alphabet. Aristophanes, too, in more than one of his plays shows that it was the ancient practice to combine these subjects in the education of boys, and in Menander's play *The Changeling*, the old man, in explaining to the father who is claiming his son the items of expenditure incurred in the boy's education, says that he has paid large sums to musicians and teachers of geometry.

19. This, too, was the origin of the ancient practice of passing the lyre round at banquets after the feasting was over, and on one such occasion when Themistocles admitted that he could not play it, 'he was', to use the words of Cicero, 'accounted but ill-educated'.

20. At the banquet of the ancient Romans, too, it was customary to have music upon stringed instruments and flutes; and the verses of the dancing priests of Mars have their tunes. All these practices were instituted by Numa, and they prove conclusively that, even amongst those whom we regard as savage and warlike, music did not fail to receive all the attention which the circumstances of the age allowed.

21. Finally it passed into a familiar Greek proverb, that those who lack education have no dealings either with the Graces or with the Muses.

22. But let us now explain the advantages which the future orator may look for from the study of music, in his own peculiar sphere.

Music has two modes of expression, viz. through vocal utterance, and through the gestures of the body, in both of which the orator aims at a certain fitting harmony. The theory of vocal utterance is divided by the musician Aristoxenus into rhythmic and metric, the former concerned with the modulation of the voice, the latter with melody and the actual sounds produced. Are not all these things, then, necessary for the orator? One has a bearing upon gesture, another upon arrangement of words, and a third upon the inflexions of the voice which in pleading, as elsewhere, extend over an extremely wide range.

23. The alternative view would be that it is only in songs and the lyrical portions of comedy that structure and the smooth joining of words are demanded, but that in pleading these things are unnecessary, or else that arrangement and melody are not employed in a speech as they are in music to suit the requirements of the material in hand.

24. In the case of singing by utterance and by modulation sublimity is given to noble themes, sweetness to pleasant ones, and smoothness to passages that lack emotion, and the whole art of music lies in the sympathetic expression of the moods attendant upon the words which are sung.

25. And yet in pleading, too, the raising or dropping of the voice and its inflexions all aim at rousing certain feelings in the audience, and we seek to stir now the passion now the pity of a juryman by varying modulations (to employ the same word again) of arrangement and of utterance, knowing that instruments that lack the power of speech can bring men's minds under the influence of entirely different emotions.

26. Again, fitting and seemly movements of the body, called by the Greeks εὐρυθμία, are necessary for the orator and can only be learned from music. No small

portion of the art of pleading lies in the skilful use of gesture, and I have set aside a special part of my work for that subject.

27. Come, now, is it not the case that the orator will give attention, first and foremost, to his voice? And what is so peculiarly within the province of music? We must not, however, anticipate this part of the subject either: let us in the meantime be content with a single example, that of Gaius Gracchus, the foremost orator of his age, who when he was making speeches had standing behind him a musician with a pitch-pipe (τονάριον in Greek) to give him the notes to which his voice had to be attuned.

28. This he was careful to do, even in his wildest harangues, not only in those earliest days, when he struck terror into the aristocrats, but afterwards, too, when he came to be afraid of them.

For the sake of less learned critics, 'men of a duller Muse', as the saying goes, I should like to remove all doubts as to the usefulness of the study of music.

29. Surely they will admit that the budding orator must read the poets. But surely this is not possible without some knowledge of music? Even if one is blind enough mentally to be doubtful about other kinds of poetry, the necessity will at least be admitted in the case of the lyrical poets. This argument would require to be developed, if I were advocating this as a new study.

30. But since it has been recognized from early times, from the days of Chiron and Achilles right down to our own, amongst all who have not shirked the normal course of education, it is not for me to cast doubts upon its value by too anxious a defence.

31. It will, I believe, be sufficiently clear from the examples just quoted what sort of music I approve and to what extent, but still I think I ought to declare even more explicitly that I do not recommend the music of the modern stage, effeminate as it is and feeble in its wanton measures, a type of music which has gone far towards robbing us of any manly vigour that still remained in our midst; what I recommend is the music in which the praises of brave men were sung and in which brave men sang themselves in days gone by. Nor would I have my pupils play upon those psalteries and lutes which no modest maiden would ever handle, but I wish them to acquire a knowledge of those laws of harmony, which are so useful in stirring and in soothing the emotions.

32. It is recorded that once when certain youths had been worked up to the point of assaulting with violence a respectable home, Pythagoras bade the musician change her strain to a slow spondaic measure, and in that way succeeded in calming their passions. Chrysippus, too, assigns a tune of an appropriate character to the lullaby sung by nurses to soothe young children.

33. There is also a theme for declamation in the schools, invented with considerable ingenuity, in which a flute-player figures, who had played a Phrygian tune to a priest at a sacrifice and when the priest was driven mad and threw himself over a cliff, was brought to trial as being responsible for his death. Now if such a case is worthy of a pleader's skill and if it cannot be handled without a knowledge of music, how can even the most unfriendly critics fail to admit that this art too is necessary for our purpose?

Geometry

34. In the case of geometry the critics allow that some training is useful for pupils of tender years: for they admit that by this study minds are kept active, wits sharpened, and the power of observation quickened, but they imagine that its value lies, not like that of other studies in the knowledge which results from learning, but in the process of learning itself. (Such is the common view.)

35. It is not, however, without good reason that most eminent men have directed especial care to this branch of knowledge

Geometry is divided into two portions, concerned respectively with numbers and with figures. Now a knowledge of numbers is necessary not only for the orator but for every one who has the least smattering of letters. In pleading, such knowledge is constantly in request, and if the pleader, I do not say betrays uneasiness about the results of his calculations, but even hints by any uncertain or fumbling movement of his fingers that he is not quite sure about the calculations themselves, he is accounted a man of little education.

36. The theory of linear figures, too, is constantly cropping up in legal cases (for law suits are concerned with boundaries and measurements), but geometry has another and a more important relationship with the art of oratory.

37. In the first place, logical sequence is required in geometry: is it not also required in eloquence?

Geometry proves what follows from prior data, the unknown from the known: do we not do that in speaking? Nay, does not the familiar demonstration of geometrical propositions consist almost entirely of syllogisms? That is why you will find many who hold that this art (geometry) is more akin to dialectic than to rhetoric. But the orator, too, though rarely, will use the dialectical form of proof.

38. As for syllogisms, he will use them if the occasion demands it, and he will certainly employ the rhetorical form of syllogisms called the enthymeme. Finally, the most rigid proofs are those commonly styled 'geometrical demonstrations'. But what is the aim of an oration if it be not proof?

39. Geometrical reasoning is also employed to detect fallacies which though specious are untrue. This is also done in the case of numbers by means of the so-called ψευδογραφίαι, with which we used to amuse ourselves when we were boys. But there are more important instances. Who, for example, would not assent to this proposition: 'If the boundaries which enclose spaces are equal in length, the areas enclosed within these boundaries must also be equal'?

40. The proposition, however, is untrue. For it makes a vital difference what the shape of the enclosing boundary is, and the geometers have justly censured the historians who believed that the size of islands is sufficiently indicated by the length of the voyage round their shores. As a matter of fact, the enclosed area is greatest when the figure formed by the periphery is most perfect.

41. Thus, if the boundary line forms a circle, the most perfect of plane figures, it will enclose a greater area than if it makes a square, and, again, squares will enclose greater areas than triangles and equilateral triangles greater areas than triangles whose sides are not equal.

42. In case other examples should prove rather difficult, let us take an instance that is perfectly easy even for the ignorant.

There is scarcely any one who does not know that a juger of land measures two hundred and forty feet in length and half that in breadth, and it is a simple matter to calculate its circumference and its area.

43. But a square with sides of one hundred and eighty feet each has the same total periphery, but encloses a much larger area within its four sides. If any one shirks making the required calculation, he may learn the same truth from smaller figures. A square with sides of ten feet each will have a periphery of forty feet and an area of one hundred square feet. But a rectangle with sides of fifteen feet and ends of five feet will with the same periphery have only three-fourths of the area enclosed in the square.

44. And if the sides of the rectangle are nineteen feet long and the ends one foot each, the number of square feet enclosed will be the same as the number of feet in the sides, viz. nineteen. But the periphery will be equal to that of the square, which contains a hundred square feet. Thus, the farther you depart from the form of the square the greater the loss in area enclosed.

45. So it may even come about that with a greater periphery you may have a smaller area. This applies to plane figures. In the case of hills and valleys it is obvious even to the ignorant that the area of the ground is greater than that of the sky above it.

46. And what of the fact that this same science of geometry rises even to the explanation of the laws which control the universe? And as it teaches us by numerical

calculation that the courses of the stars are fixed and established, we learn in the course of this study that nothing is haphazard and a mere matter of chance: a lesson which may sometimes be of importance to the orator.

47. To take an example, when the Athenians were terror-stricken by an eclipse of the sun, and Pericles reassured them by explaining the causes of the phenomenon, or when the famous Sulpicius Gallus in the army of Lucius Paulus held forth on the subject of lunar eclipse, that the minds of the soldiers might not be filled with fear at what might seem a miracle wrought by supernatural agencies, do not both these men appear to have exercised the functions of an orator?

48. If Nicias in Sicily had possessed such knowledge he would not have been overcome by the same sort of panic and lost the splendid Athenian army. On a similar occasion, when Dion advanced to overthrow the tyranny of Dionysius, he was not deterred by such an occurrence. We may grant that the uses of such knowledge in war are outside our purview, and pass over the case of Archimedes, who singlehanded prolonged considerably the siege of Syracuse.

49. But this, at any rate, is relevant to our purpose, that many questions which it is more difficult to explain by any other method are usually dealt with by means of geometrical demonstration, e.g. the theory of ordinary and of infinite division, and the question of acceleration. And so, if an orator has to speak on every kind of subject, as my second book will prove, it is impossible for any one to be an orator without a knowledge of geometry.

CHAPTER 11

ELEMENTARY INSTRUCTION IN SPEECH AND GESTURE

1. SOME attention must also be given to the comic actor, at least in so far as the future orator seeks a knowledge of delivery. For I have no desire that the boy whom we are training for this career should acquire the broken shrillness of a woman's voice or the trembling accents of old age.

2. Nor ought he to ape the faulty utterance of drunkenness, nor be imbued with the insolence of a familiar slave, nor learn to express the emotions of love, avarice, and fear. These things are not necessary for an orator, and they taint the mind while it is still peculiarly susceptible and unformed in the earliest years, for constant imitation passes into habit.

3. Nor are all his gestures and movements to be borrowed from the actor on the comic stage. For although the orator ought to employ both up to a point, yet he will be very different indeed from a player, shunning extravagance in expression, in gesture, and in movement. For if there is any art in these particulars which orators employ, it is first and foremost to conceal its existence as art.

4. What, then, is the duty of this teacher? First of all, let him correct any defects of speech which may exist, so that words may be pronounced clearly and each letter enunciated with its correct sound. For we get into difficulties through undue shrillness or thickness in pronouncing certain letters; some we fail to accent sharply enough, substituting sounds not unlike them, but duller.

5. Thus the letter rho (R), with which Demosthenes, too, found difficulty, is replaced by lambda (L)—we have the same sounds in Latin—and again when C and G are mispronounced they are softened into T and D.

6. Further, this teacher will not put up with any affectation in pronouncing S, nor will he allow words to be uttered deep down in the throat or to re-echo from the open mouth; nor will he suffer a practice which ill befits purity of speech, that of enveloping simple natural utterance in an artificial drawl which the Greeks describe as καταπεπλασμένον.

7. This is the name given to the sound of flutes whose treble stops are closed and which give forth a deeper note issuing directly from the end of the instrument.

8. He will also see to it that final syllables are not clipped, that our speech is uniform in quality, that when emphasis is necessary the effort is one of lungs and not of head, that gesture is suited to voice and expression to gesture.

9. Care must also be taken that the speaker look straight before him, that his lips be not twisted, that too wide an opening of the mouth do not keep the jaws agape, that the head be not thrown back too far, the eyes not fixed upon the ground, the neck not bent to this side or to that.

10. The face, too, may err in several ways. I have seen many whose eyebrows were raised at each stress of the voice, others with brows contracted in a constant frown, others whose eyebrows disagree, one turned up to the top of the head, the other almost concealing the eye beneath it.

11. But, as I shall show later, infinite importance

attaches to these details and nothing can please that is unbecoming.

12. The actor must also teach our pupil how a story is told, with what authoritative utterance one must urge a course of action, the animation that shows rising anger, the modulation that befits a show of pity. And this he will do best by choosing from comedies special passages, those best suited for this purpose, i.e. those which most closely resemble pleadings.

13. Not only will these prove most useful as exercises in delivery: they will also be well calculated to foster eloquence.

14. Such must be our pupil's training while he is too young to profit by more serious instruction. But when he has to read speeches and can at length appreciate their merits, then I would have at his side a skilful and conscientious teacher, not only to mould his style in reading but also to compel him to learn by heart selected passages and to deliver them in a clear voice and standing up just as he will have to do in court. Thus he will gain practice from the first in delivery, in voice production, and in the use of memory.

15. Neither do I regard as blameworthy those who also devote a brief space to teachers of gymnastic. I do not mean those who give up part of their lives to anointing themselves with oil for wrestling, part to excessive drinking of wine—men who destroy the mind by too much attention to the body (such men I would keep as far away as possible from our pupil).

16. But the same name belongs to those who mould gestures and movements, so that the arms are held straight, the hands betray no awkwardness or clumsiness, the pose is graceful, the movement of the feet

appropriate, and the head and eyes in harmony with the whole poise of the body.

17. All men agree that these things belong to the art of delivery, and associate delivery with the orator. And assuredly we must not disdain to learn what must be done, especially as the 'chironomia', which, as its name indicates, is the law of gesture, originated in the good old days, won the approval of the most eminent men in Greece, including Socrates himself, was placed among a citizen's accomplishments by Plato, and was not forgotten by Chrysippus in his precepts concerning education.

18. It is recorded that the Spartans even included in their exercises a certain type of dancing as being useful in training men for war. Nor did the Romans of old regard dancing as disgraceful, witness its survival in the name of the dancing priests and in religious ritual, witness also the words of Crassus in the third book of Cicero's *De Oratore*, in which he urges the orator to employ 'robust and manly movements of the body, borrowed not from actors and the stage, but from the camp or even from the wrestling school'. Training of this type has remained customary until this day, and no one has raised his voice against it.

19. I shall not, however, retain it after boyhood's years, nor for a great length of time even then. For I would not have an orator's gestures as studied as a dancer's movements: all I desire is that something should remain from this youthful training to give us, though we are unconscious of it, that grace of action which learners consciously acquire.

CHAPTER 12

CAN BOYS BE TAUGHT A NUMBER OF SUBJECTS AT THE SAME TIME?

1. The question is often asked, whether, granting that these things should be learned, they can all be taught and acquired at one and the same time. This some deny, holding that the mind is confused and wearied by many subjects of diverse import, for which there is neither mental nor bodily strength nor sufficient time; holding, too, that, no matter how true it is that pupils of maturer age can endure the toil, the years of childhood should not be burdened.

2. These critics, however, do not realize the strength of the human mind, which is so swift and agile, so all-embracing, if I may say so, in its outlook that it cannot limit itself to a single object, but directs its energy to several, not merely on the same day but at the same moment of time.

3. Is it not the case that performers on the harp attend at the same time to the music they have to remember, to the sound of the voice, and to its countless modulations, while with the right hand they run over certain strings and with the left strike others, stop, or release them? The foot, too, is not idle, but maintains the regular beat of the music, and all these things are done simultaneously.

4. Again, do not we pleaders, when we are called suddenly, say certain things while we are thinking of others to follow, attending at the same time to the selection of arguments, the choice of words, arrangement, gesture, delivery, facial expression, and movements of the body? And if these in all their diversity

are, as it were, the product of a single effort, why should we not divide our hours of study among a number of different subjects? Especially as change of occupation in itself refreshes and restores the mind, while, on the other hand, it is considerably more difficult to concentrate for long upon a single task. Thus reading affords a respite from writing and the monotony of reading is relieved by changes of subject.

5. However much we have done already, yet we are in a measure fresh for what we are starting upon. Who could help being jaded, if he had to listen all day long to one teacher of a subject—no matter what? He will be refreshed by change just as, in the case of food, variety refreshes the stomach and nourishes us without that distaste which monotony of diet must arouse.

6. Or else let those critics show me an alternative method of learning. Are we to devote ourselves entirely to the grammarian, then to the teacher of geometry, dropping now what we learnt before? Are we then to pass on to the music master, our previous studies forgotten? And when we study Latin literature, are we to ignore Greek? In a word, are we to do nothing but what we took up last?

7. Why do we not give the same advice to farmers, bidding them not to grow vines, olives, and orchard trees at the same time, not to tend meadowlands, stock, gardens, beehives, and poultry? Why do we ourselves assign each day a certain time to business in the forum, so much to the needs of friends, so much to family responsibilities, so much to exercise, and so much to pleasure? Any one of these things would weary us if pursued uninterruptedly. So much easier is it to do many things than to do one for a long time.

8. There is, indeed, no need to fear that boys will find it difficult to endure the toil of study. For no age is less susceptible to fatigue. This may perhaps be surprising, but you can prove it by experiment: the mind is more receptive before it sets hard.

9. This is clearly proved by the fact that within two years of a child's being able to form words correctly he speaks practically the whole language without any one urging him on. Yet for how many years do our imported slaves wrestle with the Latin language?

If you start teaching reading to an adult, you may appreciate the reason for describing those who excel in their own arts as παιδομαθεῖς (i.e. taught young).

10. Again, a boy's nature is better fitted to endure toil than a young man's. Clearly, just as the bodies of young children take less harm than would an adult's from their constant falling on the ground, their creeping on hands and knees, and, later on, their constant games and running about all day long, because they are light and no burden to themselves, so their minds, too, I suppose, because they move with less effort and apply themselves to study without forcing their own initiative, simply allowing themselves to be moulded passively, do not feel the same measure of fatigue.

11. Moreover, in accordance with the general adaptability of youth, they follow their teachers without question and do not measure the progress already made, and indeed they are as yet without any sort of critical judgement as regards their work. Further, as we have often found, the senses are less affected by hard work than by hard thinking.

12. But there will never be more time for study (than in childhood), because at that age all progress

depends upon what is heard from teachers. When the pupil goes apart to write, when he creates and composes something himself, then he will have either no time or no inclination to begin these studies.

13. Therefore, seeing that the grammarian cannot and ought not to take up the whole day, to what other studies shall we by preference assign these odds and ends of time?

14. I have no desire that our pupil should be wholly absorbed in these pursuits: he need not play or set songs to music, nor need he go into the most subtle intricacies of geometry. It is not a comic actor in his delivery or a dancer in his gestures that I am fashioning. Yet even if I were to demand complete proficiency there would still be time. For the age of learning is long and I am not speaking of dullards.

15. Finally, why was Plato pre-eminent in all these things which, as I think, ought to be studied by the future orator? Because he was not content with the training which Athens could give or with that of the Pythagoreans which he had sailed to Italy to seek, but also visited the priests of Egypt and mastered all their mysterious lore.

16. We make the plea of difficulty a cloak for our own laziness. For we have no love of work, nor is eloquence sought after in itself as being honourable and the purest of all things, but we gird ourselves for base purposes and for the amassing of ignoble wealth.

17. Many a man may speak in the forum without the training I have sketched and pocket his fee, but may he be less wealthy than the base huckster and may the auctioneer make more out of the use of his voice. I would not even wish my book to be read by one who calculates what this training will bring him in.

18. But he who by a measure of divine inspiration has formed in his mind a true vision of eloquence, who sets before his eyes what a great poet calls 'oratory, queen of the world', and who seeks his reward not in the fees his cases bring him in but in his own mind in the joy of contemplation and of knowledge, a lasting reward that is not the sport of fortune—such a man will easily persuade himself to spend upon geometry and music the hours that are wasted (by others) on shows, on games in the campus, on dice, on idle talk, to say nothing of sleep and long-drawn-out banquets, realizing as he will do how much more real enjoyment he will have in these studies than in such boorish forms of pleasure. For heaven has bestowed upon many this blessing, that they find their greatest pleasures in the noblest things.

19. But we have ourselves been carried away by this sweet delight. So much for the studies wherein the boy must be grounded before he passes on to higher things. The next book will make a fresh start, and pass to the duties of the teacher of rhetoric.

BOOK II

CHAPTER 1

WHEN SHOULD THE PUPIL PASS ON TO THE SCHOOL OF RHETORIC?

1. It has been a common practice in the past, and it is one which is daily gaining ground, that pupils should be handed over to the teachers of eloquence at a later stage than reason demands: this is always the case with Latin rhetoric and it sometimes happens with Greek rhetoric also. The reason is twofold: first, that our teachers of rhetoric, at any rate, have abandoned their proper function, and second, that grammarians have exceeded theirs.

2. The teachers of rhetoric consider it their duty only to declaim and to instruct in the theory and practice of declamation, limiting it to deliberative and judicial oratory and considering all else beneath the dignity of their calling; while the grammarians, not content with that portion of the field which was appropriately left to them (and for their activities in which we owe them a debt of gratitude), encroach upon declamation in character and upon deliberative themes, wherein the burden of speaking is a very heavy one indeed.

3. Thus it comes to pass that what are properly the initial stages of a higher training become the last stages of the lower, and an age which ought to be devoted to more advanced studies remains on the level of the lower school and practises rhetoric with the grammarians, the ridiculous result being that a boy

does not seem ready to be sent to the master of declamation until he knows how to declaim.

4. Let us assign to each calling its proper limits, and let 'grammar' or 'literature', to give it its Latin name, recognize its boundaries, especially as it has passed so far beyond the modest sphere which its name indicates and to which its original teachers confined themselves. Starting as a tiny stream, it has absorbed the strength of poets and historians and now flows as a river broad enough to fill a deep channel, for besides the theory of correct speech, in itself no shallow rivulet, it includes a study of practically all the most important branches of human knowledge.

5. On the other hand, let rhetoric, which owes its name to the power of speaking well, not renounce its duties or rejoice to see its proper task encroached upon; in giving up its proper work it has almost lost its heritage.

6. I shall not, of course, deny that a grammarian may possess sufficient knowledge to be able to teach rhetoric as well, but when he does so he fulfils the function of a rhetorician and not his own.

7. We now proceed to inquire when a boy may be considered ready to learn what rhetoric teaches. Here we ought not to consider the pupil's age, but rather how far he has advanced in his studies. And, not to waste time on discussing when he is to be handed over to the teacher of rhetoric, I think the best way of settling the matter is simply to say, 'when he is ready for it'. But this, of course, is wrapped up with the question we have just discussed.

8. If the function of the grammarian is extended to include deliberative speaking, the need for the rhetor

will come later; if the rhetor does not refuse what are really the elementary portions of his task, his guidance is required as soon as the boy starts upon narratives and little compositions conveying praise or blame.

9. We know that amongst the ancients it was a favourite type of exercise for the improvement of eloquence to speak on general topics and commonplaces without involving particular events and persons, as must happen in real or imaginary cases. From this it is clear how scandalously the teaching of rhetoric now neglects what was its first and for many a day its only subject-matter.

10. What is there in the exercises above mentioned which does not fall within the peculiar province of rhetoric and even within the narrower sphere of forensic eloquence? Do we not have to narrate in court? I rather think that is what we have to do more often than anything else.

11. Is not praise or blame frequently made a feature of such contests? As for commonplaces, either those that are directed against vices such as Cicero is said to have composed or those in which questions are handled in a general way, e.g. those published by Quintus Hortensius on such topics as 'should we attach importance to small pieces of evidence?' or 'on behalf of witnesses' or 'against witnesses'—are not these, I say, a portion of the very marrow of lawsuits?

12. These are in a way weapons which should always be at hand that we may use them when occasion arises. He who considers that they do not concern oratory will not believe that the making of a statue has begun when its limbs are being cast: and further, let no one find fault with what some critics will consider

my undue haste, as though I held that the pupil thus handed over to the rhetor is to be taken away altogether from the grammarians.

13. To them, too, set times will be assigned, nor need we fear lest the boy be overburdened with two teachers. For his task will not be increased, but merely divided, whereas formerly it was combined in the hands of one master. Each will be more efficient in his own department. This practice still holds with the Greeks, but has been abandoned by the Latin teachers of rhetoric, excusably, perhaps, since others have been found to undertake their duties.

CHAPTER 2

THE CHARACTER AND RESPONSIBILITIES OF THE TEACHER

1. WHEN the boy has reached in his studies a degree of advancement which enables him to grasp what we have indicated as the first steps in rhetorical instruction, he must be handed over to the teachers of that art. It is of especial importance that the moral character of these teachers should be considered.

2. I am led to emphasize this point here, not because I attach no importance to the matter in the case of other teachers, too (witness what I said in the preceding book), but because the very age of the pupils makes it more necessary to mention it.

3. Pupils are transferred to the school of rhetoric when they are practically grown up, and they continue there when they are young men; accordingly, we must at this stage exercise even greater care that the stainless character of the teacher may preserve their more tender years from harm and that the weight of his authority may deter their bolder age from excess.

4. It is not enough that he should himself show rigid self-control, he must also by the strictness of his discipline control the behaviour of the pupils who gather round him. Let him, then, above all things adopt the attitude of a parent toward his pupils and consider that he is taking the place of those who entrust their children to him.

5. He must have no vices himself and tolerate none in his pupils. Let him be stern but not melancholy, friendly but not familiar, lest in the one case he incur

dislike, in the other contempt. He must constantly dwell upon the honourable and the good; for the more he admonishes his pupils the less he will require to punish them. He must never lose his temper, yet he will not pass over what deserves correction; he must be simple in his teaching, able to endure hard toil, persevering rather than exacting.

6. He must answer questions readily and put questions himself to those who do not ask them. In praising the recitations of his pupils he must not be either niggardly or extravagant, for in the former case he will arouse a distaste for toil, in the latter a spirit of self-complacency.

7. In correcting faults he will not be harsh and never abusive; for many are driven away from the studies they have entered upon by the fact that some teachers find fault as though they hated the offender.

8. Every day he must himself recite something, nay, many things, that his hearers can carry away with them. For though he may supply them with abundant material for imitation from the books they are reading, yet what is termed the living voice gives richer nourishment, especially if it be the voice of a teacher whom pupils, provided they are rightly trained, both love and respect. It is wellnigh impossible to say how much more readily we imitate those for whom we have a liking.

9. The common custom of allowing boys to stand up and shout their applause is not at all a proper one. Young people, when they are listening to others, ought to express their feelings in a modest fashion. Thus the pupil will rely upon the judgement of his teacher and believe that he has recited well when he wins the teacher's approval.

10. The vicious practice which nowadays goes by the name of politeness, whereby everything good or bad is praised in turn, is not only unseemly and more worthy of the theatre than of the stern discipline of a school, but also a deadly foe to real study. For care and toil seem superfluous when praise awaits no matter what effusion.

11. The audience, then, just as much as the reciter should keep their eyes upon the teacher's face: for thus what is good will be distinguished from what is bad, and if writing gives fluency, listening gives the power of judgement.

12. As it is, the boys lean forward girt for the fray and at every period not merely rise but even dart out of their places and shout their applause with unseemly din. The compliment is a mutual one, and this is the reward of the reciter. The result is pride and vain self-conceit, so much so that, puffed up by this tumultuous demonstration on the part of their fellow students, they feel aggrieved if the master is not also lavish in his praise.

13. Teachers, too, should insist upon attention and modest behaviour in those who listen to their declamations: for the master ought not to speak to suit the taste of his pupils, but vice versa. Nay, he should, if possible, pay careful attention and observe what each pupil praises and how he praises it, and rejoice that his good points win approval not more for his own sake than for the sake of those who duly appreciate them.

14. I do not approve of boys and young men sitting together. For though such a teacher as ought to be in charge of their studies and their morals can maintain proper discipline even among grown youths, yet the

weaker should be kept apart from the stronger and not merely the charge but even the suspicion of immorality avoided.

15. These points I thought ought to be noted briefly. As for grosser vices, I do not think it necessary even to warn the teacher that both he and his school should be free from them. And if there is any one who in choosing a teacher for his son does not avoid manifest evil, let him be assured that through this omission all the other rules which we are trying to lay down for the guidance of youth are rendered null and void.

CHAPTER 3

SHOULD WE EMPLOY THE BEST TEACHER TO INSTRUCT BEGINNERS?

1. We ought not to pass over in silence the view of those who, even when they consider boys ready for the school of rhetoric, think they ought not to be handed over right away to the most distinguished teacher, but keep them for a while with the less eminent teachers, on the ground that a master of mediocre talent is more suited for the task of imparting instruction in the arts, since he is easier to understand and imitate and less inclined to be intolerant of the drudgery of elementary teaching.

2. I do not think it would take long to prove how much better it is to be grounded in the best principles, and how difficult it is to eradicate faults that have once taken firm root: it means that a double load is placed upon the shoulders of the next teacher, and to undo faulty teaching is harder than to teach aright.

3. That is why the famous musician Timotheus is said to have been in the habit of demanding double fees from those who had been under other teachers as compared with those who came to him entirely untaught. The view to which I have just referred is at fault in two respects. In the first place, these people imagine that inferior teachers are good enough in the meantime, and are content because they can put up with any sort of mental food;

4. and though such carelessness is in itself worthy of censure, it would none the less be endurable if such instructors merely fell short in quantity and not in

quality. The second misapprehension is a commoner one: people think that those who possess richer gifts of eloquence do not condescend to elementary instruction, partly because they have a distaste for the drudgery of the lower studies and partly because they cannot teach them.

5. For myself, I do not consider one who will not descend to these levels a teacher at all, and I maintain that the best orator, if he will, is best able to impart such instruction. First, because it is reasonable to expect that one who surpasses all others in eloquence has also the best understanding of those elements through which eloquence is attained;

6. second, because in teaching method is all important, and the most learned men possess it in the highest degree; and lastly, because no one is great in the higher branches of a subject if he lacks a sound foundation in the elements. Unless perchance Phidias made a matchless Jove, but another artist would have executed the detailed ornamentation of the work better than he, or an orator will not know how to pronounce words, or an eminent physician be unable to cure trifling ailments.

7. What, then? Is there no higher eloquence too great for the feeble minds of boys to understand? There is indeed: but our eloquent instructor will have to be wise as well, and know the principles of teaching, coming down to the level of his pupil, as a swift walker, if he happens to be walking with a child, gives him his hand and shortens his stride, and does not go too fast for his small companion.

8. Moreover, it is usually the case that the instruction of the most learned is easier to understand and far

more lucid. The first virtue of eloquence is clearness, and the weaker a man's talent the more he strives to raise himself and to puff himself out, as those who are of small stature rise on tiptoe and as weak men bluster.

9. Those whose style is pompous, vicious, high-sounding, and full of other forms of affectation suffer, as I think, not from excess of strength but rather of weakness, like bodies swollen not with health but with disease, or weary travellers ever straying from the straight road. Thus the worse a man's eloquence the less easy he will be to follow.

10. I have not forgotten that in the preceding book, while maintaining that learning at school is better than instruction in the home, I said that in the elementary stages, when but little progress has been made, pupils are more easily fired to imitate their fellow-pupils because such emulation is easier: a point which some may take as though it meant that I am now contradicting my earlier view. Far from it.

11. It is the best possible reason for handing over a boy to the best teachers that with them the pupils, being better taught, will either say what is worth imitating or will be corrected at once, if they make a mistake. But the ignorant teacher will perhaps even give his approval to what is faulty and through his judgement upon it commend it to his hearers.

12. The teacher, then, should be outstanding alike in eloquence and moral character, able like Phoenix in Homer to teach his pupils both how to speak and how to act.

CHAPTER 4

THE FIRST EXERCISES IN THE SCHOOL OF RHETORIC

1. I SHALL now begin to explain what I regard as the first duties of the teachers of rhetoric, postponing for a little consideration of that which alone is commonly styled the art of rhetoric. And it seems to me that we can best begin with what resembles the instruction already received by the pupil in the school of the grammarian.

2. There are three recognized types of narrative (excluding that used in pleading): *the fable*, which is found in tragedies and epic poems, removed not only from fact but also from all resemblance to fact, *the fictitious narrative*, used in comedy, and, though not true to fact, yet resembling it, and *historical narrative*, consisting in the exposition of actual occurrences. The poetical types we have assigned to the grammarians: in the school of rhetoric, a beginning should be made with history, which is the more forceful in proportion to its greater degree of truth.

3. What we regard as the best method of narrating will be expounded when we come to deal with judicial narrative. In the meantime it is enough to warn the beginner that it must not be wholly dry and lifeless (for why need we devote so much labour to our study of it if it seemed enough to state facts baldly without adornment?), nor, on the other hand, wantonly involved and full of far-fetched descriptions, faults to which many become liable through imitating the freedom of poetry.

4. Both extremes are bad: the former, however, is the

worse, arising as it does from barrenness rather than from superabundance. In boys we cannot demand or even hope for finished eloquence; yet there is more virtue in a rich endowment and noble aspirations and a spirit which in its inexperience yearns to reach the unattainable.

5. Nor would I ever in a pupil of this age be offended by undue exuberance: nay, rather I would have teachers themselves solicitous to nourish somewhat tenderly, as nurses would, minds that are still plastic and suffer them to drink their fill, so to say, of the milk of the humaner studies. Whereby the body will for the nonce wax plumper, which ere long maturer years are to reduce.

6. Thus we may hope for strength to come: whereas a child that in infancy shows all his limbs clearly defined is wont to threaten leanness and feebleness in future years. Let this age then be bold oft-times, inventive too and prone to delight in its own inventions, though they may still be lacking in exactness and clear-cut outline. It is easy to correct exuberance, but barrenness no toil can overcome.

7. Least hopeful to my mind of childish natures is that in which natural endowment is prematurely curbed by judgement. The first requirement I would seek is raw material, superabundant if you will, and lacking in due restraint. The passing of the years will refine it much, much will reason file away, somewhat by use itself will, so to say, be rubbed off, only let there be something from which cutting and carving is possible, and this there will be if we have not from the beginning drawn the plate too thin, so that deep cutting is bound to pierce it through.

8. Such a view concerning pupils of this age will not surprise any one who has read in Cicero: 'I wish indeed that fertility of invention should display itself in the young student.' Wherefore most of all to be avoided, and especially in the training of boys, is the barren teacher, just as a dry and sapless soil is to be avoided for seedlings that are still tender.

9. For with such a master they straightway become stunted and with gaze, so to say, fixed upon the ground, never daring to rise above the humdrum talk of every day. By them leanness is mistaken for health, and weakness for judgement, and while they are satisfied with the avoidance of faults they lapse into the very fault of lacking excellences. Wherefore to my mind, let not maturity of judgement come too soon, and let not the new wine in the vat be straightway mellow: thus will it stand the passing of the years and improve with age.

10. This point too it is worth while to urge, that youthful minds sometimes give way beneath the weight of correction excessively severe, for they become despondent and grieve and in the end conceive a hatred for their studies and, what is worst of all, in their fear of blundering everywhere, attempt nothing.

11. This is a fact familiar to the countryman, who does not think the pruning-knife should be applied to tender branches because they seem to shrink from the steel and to be unable as yet to bear a scar.

12. At this stage then most of all, the teacher must be of pleasant aspect, that corrections, harsh in any case by their very nature, may be softened by the gentle hand that administers them. He must praise this, pass over that, make changes too, giving the reasons

for them, and brighten up the whole by inserting something of his own. Sometimes, too, it will be useful for him to dictate complete models for the boy to imitate and for the present to love as though they were his own.

13. But if his composition be so careless that correction is useless, I have always found it helpful, when I have gone over the subject-matter once more, to bid him write his version of it afresh, telling him that he can do it still better: inasmuch as study delights in nothing more than in hope of better achievement.

14. But different ages call for different methods of correction, and work is to be exacted and amended in accordance with the measure of the pupil's intellectual powers. I used to tell my young pupils when they ventured something rather reckless or exuberant, that for the present I commended it, but that the time would come when I would not allow the same freedom: thus they found delight in their ability and yet were not deceived in their judgement.

15. But to return to the question from which I digressed. Narratives I would have composed with the greatest possible care. For while at first, when children are learning to speak, it is useful for them to repeat what they have heard, so as to gain fluency in speaking, and while they ought accordingly (assuredly with reason) to be compelled to retrace the steps of their story or, starting from the middle, to follow it up in either direction, but only at the teacher's knee while they can as yet do no more and are just beginning to weave words and things together—the purpose being the strengthening of memory at the earliest moment—yet when they have come to appreciate the

form of pure and correct speech, merely to babble extempore without waiting to think and scarcely even to rise from the bench, smacks surely of the ostentation of the mountebank.

16. Such performances do indeed excite the foolish pride of parents who know no better, but in the pupils themselves result in a contempt for hard work, brazen impudence, the habit of speaking very badly and practice in all the faults of style, while there is born in them a vice which many a time has ruined great attainments, a haughty self-conceit.

17. The time will come for acquiring fluency, nor will that portion of my theme be carelessly passed over. Meanwhile, it is enough if the boy has written something worthy of approval with all the care at his command and the most serious application of which his age is capable. Let him gain his practice thus until he has made it his second nature. He only will be able to reach the goal at which we are aiming, or come very near to it, who learns to speak correctly before he learns to speak quickly.

18. To narratives are added, not without advantage, the tasks of refuting and confirming them, which go by the names of ἀνασκευή and κατασκευή respectively. Further, these may be practised not only in dealing with myths and poetic fictions, but also in handling the records of history themselves: thus, if the subject of inquiry were 'whether we are to believe that a raven perched on the helmet of Valerius as he fought and struck the face and eyes of his Gallic foe with his beak and wings', there would be ample scope for argument:

19. or again, in dealing with the serpent from which tradition says that Scipio was born, or the wolf of

Romulus and the Egeria of Numa. In Greek legends there is usually a freedom of invention approaching that of poetry: often, too, questions are wont to arise about the place where, or the time when an event is said to have taken place, sometimes too about the hero of the story: thus Livy very often is in doubt and different historians adopt different views.

20. Thence gradually the pupil will begin to rise to higher themes, to praise famous men and to castigate the wicked, a task of manifold advantage, for therein the intellect is exercised upon a rich variety of subject-matter and the character is formed by the contemplation of right and wrong. Thence too comes a plenteous store of knowledge of the world and straightway furnishes with precedents most useful in all sorts of cases the pupil who will use them when occasion shall arise.

21. Hence too is derived the exercise of arguing which of two men is the better, which the worse: this, though employing like reasoning, yet gives double the subject-matter and handles not only the nature but also the measure of the vices. But as concerns the method of panegyric and its opposite, as it is the third part of the art of rhetoric, we shall lay down rules in due course.

22. *Commonplaces* (I refer to those compositions in which it is customary without reference to specific persons to declaim against vices themselves, such as adultery, gambling, lasciviousness) come directly from legal practice, and if the name of a person accused be added, become accusations; but these too are not usually handled in the purely abstract form, but are reduced to certain specific types, as when a blind

adulterer is dealt with, a poverty-stricken gambler, or an old roué. They admit too on occasion of speeches for the defence.

23. Thus we speak on the side of luxury or of love, and sometimes the pimp or the parasite is defended in such a way that we plead not for a person but for the alleged misdemeanour.

24. *Themes* are derived from a comparison of things, as for instance, 'Is life in the country or life in the town to be preferred?' or 'Does greater merit attach to the career of the lawyer or to that of the soldier?' These are marvellously well suited and most suggestive as topics for practice in speaking, and help very greatly both in the orator's business of persuasion and in the practice of the courts and in argument. The latter of the topics mentioned above is handled with the greatest eloquence by Cicero in his defence of Murena.

25. There are also those questions which pertain almost entirely to the deliberative type of oratory, e.g. 'Ought a man to marry?' or 'Ought a man to seek office in the State?' These, if we add specific names, will become deliberative orations.

26. My teachers had a type of exercise which not only was useful but which also gave us great satisfaction, viz. preparing us for conjectural cases, as when they bade us investigate and show 'Why Venus bears arms in Spartan story' or 'Why Cupid was thought of as a boy with wings and armed with arrows and a torch', and so forth, wherein we sought out the intention, a matter frequently in question in pleading. These we may class with 'chriae', i.e. moral sayings.

27. *Topics*, e.g. in the case of witnesses whether they are always to be believed, or in the case of proofs

whether even minute points of evidence are to be trusted, so clearly belong to forensic practice that some orators, distinguished holders of state offices, have taken care to have them written out and carefully committed to memory, that on any suitable occasion their impromptu utterances might be adorned by these adventitious ornaments, as we may style them.

28. By this practice, to be sure (for I cannot bear to postpone my judgement on this point), they seem to me to confess to great weakness in themselves. For how can these men find what is exactly appropriate in particular cases, which always present a varied and novel appearance? How can they answer the arguments put forward by opposing counsel or be quick to meet objections or cross-question witnesses, when even in dealing with topics which are hackneyed, and which arise in the majority of cases, they cannot follow up the most ordinary ideas save in words prepared beforehand with such care?

29. Nay, it necessarily follows that when they employ the same form of words in several different cases, they either excite distaste, like food kept in cold storage, or a sense of shame when their scanty intellectual furnishings are noted so often in the memories of their audience, furnishings which, as in a poor but ostentatious household, are worn to rags in a variety of different uses.

30. There is scarcely any commonplace which is so entirely 'common' that it can find a place in the fabric of a pleading without being woven in with some threads of the particular question at issue; otherwise it would be obvious that it has been not so much woven into the case as stitched on to it.

31. This is so either because it is different from the rest, or because in many cases it is wont to be brought in even when it is not much to the point, not because it is needed but because it has been prepared, just as some speakers for the sake of moral sentiments drag in the most long-winded passages, whereas the moral aphorism should spring from the subject-matter itself.

32. Such passages then are apposite and useful if they arise out of the case, but however beautiful these flowers of oratory may be, if they do not contribute to the winning of the case, they are at best superfluous and on occasion actually prejudicial. But this digression is already long enough.

33. *Praise and censure of the laws* demand powers of greater maturity, powers wellnigh adequate for the most exacting of the tasks imposed upon the orator. Whether this kind of exercise is better suited to the deliberative or to the controversial type of oratory depends upon the custom and law of the state in question. Thus in Greece the proposer of laws appeared before a judge, but in Rome the custom has been to argue for or against proposed laws before a meeting of the people. In both cases, however, brief statements, usually beyond controversy, are made.

34. There are three kinds of law—sacred, public, and private—a division which has a more direct bearing upon the commendation of a law if one rises as it were by successive steps, saying first that it is a law, then that it is a public law, and finally, that it is a law made to promote the worship of the gods. The usual points of controversy in these cases are such as are common to all laws.

35. Either it may be questioned whether the mover

of the proposed law has proper legal standing, as for instance in the case of Publius Clodius, whose election as tribune was attacked as being irregular, or the objection may be to the bill itself, on various grounds, whether it be perhaps alleged that notice of it was not given three weeks beforehand, or that it was proposed or is being proposed on a wrong day, or in defiance of the veto of another magistrate, or of the auspices, or of some other legal obstacle, or again that it is in conflict with some existing law.

36. But these points have no bearing upon the elementary exercises with which we are dealing, exercises which do not involve particular persons, occasions, or cases. There are other points which are handled in much the same way in real and in fictitious contests of this type.

37. The alleged flaw is sought either in the wording or in the content of the bill. In the case of the wording, the question is whether it is sufficiently exact or whether there is any ambiguity in it; in the case of the content, whether the proposal is consistent with itself, or whether it ought to be retrospective, or whether it should apply to particular individuals only. But the most usual point at issue is whether it is honourable or expedient.

38. I am well aware that most authorities on this point make further subdivisions, but under the term honourable we include what is just, dutiful, righteous, and the like. The various forms of justice, however, are not as a rule dismissed in a single category. For either the question concerns the action itself with which the law deals, whether it deserves punishment or reward, or it concerns the amount of the reward or punishment which may be blamed either as too great or as too small.

39. Expediency too is determined sometimes by the nature of the law, sometimes by the attendant circumstances. A favourite point of debate is whether certain measures can be enforced. Our pupils must remember too that laws are criticized sometimes as a whole, sometimes in part; examples of both kinds are afforded us in famous orations.

40. I do not forget that there are also laws not passed for all time, but dealing with civil offices or military commands—the Manilian Law for instance, which is the subject of one of Cicero's speeches. But as regards these, no instruction can be given at this point; they are composed with a view to the peculiar circumstances with which they deal and without any common principle.

41. Such, more or less, were the exercises by which the ancients developed the powers of their budding orators, borrowing, however, from the logicians their method of argument. It is pretty well admitted that among the Greeks it was in the school of Demetrius of Phalerum that the practice arose of speaking upon topics fashioned to resemble those of the market-place and of the council-chamber.

42. Whether he invented this kind of exercise, as I have confessed in another book, I do not know; even those who maintain this most strenuously have no sufficient authority to rely upon. But that Latin teachers of oratory began to use these exercises in the last years of the life of Lucius Crassus is vouched for by Cicero, and Plotius was the most distinguished of them.

CHAPTER 5

THE READING OF ORATORS AND HISTORIANS IN THE SCHOOL OF RHETORIC

1. THE method of declamation I shall deal with a little later; meanwhile, as we are discussing the first elements of rhetoric, it seems to me that I ought to take care to remind you how greatly the teacher of rhetoric will contribute to the progress of his pupils if, as the grammarian is required to expound the poets, so he trains the boys under his care in the reading of history and still more of oratory: this I did myself in the case of a few of my pupils whose age demanded it and whose parents thought it useful.

2. But though even then I felt that it was an excellent training, two things hindered me; first, the fact that long-established custom prescribed a different method of teaching; and second, the fact that those who were modelling themselves upon me were for the most part well-developed young men who did not require this type of exercise.

3. Yet even if I had discovered something new ever so late in my career, I should not be ashamed to advocate it for the future. Now I am well aware that this practice holds amongst Greek teachers of rhetoric, though usually the work is done by assistants, since it does not appear that time would suffice if the rhetoricians themselves wished to take these lessons with all their pupils individually.

4. And, indeed, the method of reading these authors with pupils which obtains—intended as it is to enable boys to follow the written word easily and clearly—

and even that which expounds the meaning of any unusual word that occurs, we must regard as far beneath the dignity of the teacher of rhetoric.

5. But to point out excellences in these authors, or on occasion defects, does form an essential part of his duty and of the profession in virtue of which he claims to be a master of eloquence, and the more so as I do not demand of teachers that they should call individual pupils to their knees and toil at the reading of whatever book each one may fancy.

6. It seems to me not only easier but also far more useful that the teacher, when he has called for silence, should set up some one pupil as a reader (it is best that this duty be assigned to the pupils in turn) that they may straightway become accustomed to enunciate clearly.

7. Then, after explaining the case for which the speech about to be read was written (for thus what is to be said will be more clearly understood), he must leave nothing unnoticed which is to be noted either in the composition or in the delivery of the speech, the method of enlisting the sympathy of the jury in the opening passage, the brilliance, brevity, and sincerity of the exposition, the design in certain passages, the hidden cunning;

8. for the only true art in oratory is not to be detected save by a craftsman himself; next he must point out the care and skill shown in the division of the subject-matter, the subtle and repeated use of argument, the strength with which the orator fires his hearers, the pleasing manner in which he soothes them, the bitterness of his taunts, the polished ease of his jests, and finally, his mastery of the emotions whereby he reaches

the heart and wins the minds of the jury to the point of view he is expounding.

9. Then, in dealing with the delivery of the speech, he must show what expressions are apt, distinguished or lofty, where fullness of treatment is praiseworthy and what is the opposite virtue, where metaphors are skilfully used, what are the figures of speech, where the construction is smooth and squared off and yet full of manly strength.

10. Another practice, too, is not without its use, viz. reading in class occasionally speeches which are inelegant and faulty, but which are admired by many whose taste is corrupt, and pointing out in these speeches the numerous examples of inappropriate or obscure treatment, of turgid or degraded utterance, of meanness, wantonness, or effeminacy. Many critics not merely praise such speeches but, what is worse, praise them just because they are corrupt.

11. For straightforward speech, naturally expressed, does not appear to be the work of genius; but what is distorted in some measure, that we praise as being more recondite, just as some people think more of bodies that are crooked or in some way monstrous than of those which have lost none of the beauties of normal formation;

12. in the same way, those who are misled by appearances think there is more beauty than uncorrupted nature can produce in people who pluck out or shave their hair or dress their tresses with hot curling-irons and are radiant with an artificial complexion, so that it would appear that beauty of person comes from depravity of manners.

13. Not only will the teacher himself be bound to

give such lessons: he will also have constantly to set questions and test the judgement of his pupils. For if they listen with such questions in view, carelessness will vanish and what is said will fall upon attentive ears. At the same time they will be led on to that which is the aim and object of their training, viz. finding things out for themselves and understanding them. For what other purpose have we in teaching but this, that our pupils may not always require teaching?

14. This kind of careful discipline, I would make bold to say, will contribute more to advancement in learning than all the text-books of all the writers upon rhetoric. Useful these books undoubtedly are, but with their wider range of application, how can they deal with all the particular appearances of things which are coming to birth almost every day?

15. Just so in the case of the military art there are certain common precepts handed down by tradition, yet it will be more useful to know on what principles each general has acted wisely or foolishly, in what circumstances, at what time, and in what place. For in almost every sphere precepts are of less value than practical experiments.

16. Or, indeed, is the teacher himself to declaim as a model for his hearers, and will not the reading of Cicero or of Demosthenes help them more? Is a pupil to be corrected in class if he has made a mistake in his declamation, and will it not be more instructive, nay pleasanter as well, to correct the speech of some one else? Assuredly, for every one prefers other people's faults to be corrected rather than his own.

17. Further arguments I had in plenty, but the usefulness of this kind of training is known to every

one, and I can only wish that there were not so much disinclination to adopt it as there will assuredly be satisfaction in having done so.

What authors should be read first?

18. If this method be adopted, there will remain the not very difficult question, 'What authors are to be read first?' Some have recommended the less famous authors as appearing easier to understand, others the more florid type as being better suited to nourish the mind of youth.

19. I myself recommend the best authors to begin with and all the time, but amongst them my preference would be for the most transparent in style and the most lucid in expression. Thus I would rather have boys read Livy than Sallust, though the latter is the greater historian, for to understand him requires a certain degree of proficiency.

20. Cicero, to my way of thinking, is a pleasant author for beginners and is sufficiently easy to understand: not only is he a useful model but he can also be loved; and after him, as Livy advises, other writers in the order of their resemblance to Cicero.

21. But there are two kinds of writing regarding which I think, for the sake of our young pupils, we must be especially on our guard: in one case we must beware lest some blind partisan of antiquity suffer them to grow hard in the reading of the Gracchi and Cato and other writers of the same sort; for they will become uncouth and spiritless: not only will they fail to grasp as yet the secret of the strength of these authors, but content to catch their manner of expression—which in those days was excellent but is unsuited to our times—

they will most disastrously imagine that they themselves resemble great men.

22. The other danger to be guarded against is the opposite one, of pupils being ensnared by the flowery conceits of our undisciplined moderns, and so falling under the spell of a corrupt kind of pleasure, with the result that they come to love that honeyed style of writing which is the more pleasing to youthful minds in proportion as it is closer to them.

23. But when their powers of judgement are fully developed and established beyond the danger of their going wrong, I would urge them to read both the old writers (for if we smooth down the roughness of an uncultured age and borrow their massive manly strength of intellect, our own polished modern style will shine forth the more brightly for it) and the moderns in whom also there is much excellence.

24. For nature has not condemned us to dullness. But we have adopted a new style of expression and given ourselves too much licence: and so it comes about that the ancients are our superiors not so much in ability as in definiteness of purpose. Thus it will be possible to choose many things for imitation (in the moderns), but we shall have to be careful that these are not contaminated by the less admirable qualities with which they are associated.

25. But, indeed, why should I not admit, nay rather insist, that there were in days gone by and are to-day certain writers who are wholly worthy of imitation.

26. Who these are it is not for every one to decide. Mistakes are actually safer in the case of the ancients, and accordingly I have postponed the reading of the moderns lest imitation should outstrip wise judgement.

CHAPTER 6

RHETORICAL DIVISION AND THE PUTTING IN HAND OF MATERIAL

1. THERE has also been a divergence in teaching method, in that some teachers, not content with laying out by division the materials which they gave their pupils for declamation, followed this up by speaking themselves at considerable length, filling out their treatment not only with summaries of evidence but also with passages of emotional appeal.

2. Some, after sketching the main outlines only, proceeded, after the declamations had been delivered, to handle particular points omitted by pupils and to polish certain passages with as much care as when they were themselves rising to speak in court. Both methods are useful and, therefore, I separate neither from the other; but if it be necessary to employ one only, it will avail more to have pointed out the right way at the outset than to recall from their straying those who have already missed the road.

3. The first reason for this is that our pupils only listen to correction, whereas division of the subject-matter is carried into their thinking and writing as well. And, again, since they hearken more willingly to instruction than to censure, if there be some a trifle high-spirited, especially with manners as they are to-day, they actually grow angry at admonition and silently fight against it.

4. Yet this is no reason why faults should not be pointed out quite frankly: for we must take account of the other pupils who will believe that everything is

right which the teacher has not corrected. The two methods must be combined and handled as circumstances in each case demand.

5. For beginners will have to be given their material sketched out, so to speak, beforehand, in accordance with the strength of each one. But when they are seen to have fashioned themselves sufficiently well after their model, they must be shown a few brief outlines only, in following which they can now, by their own strength, advance without assistance.

6. Sometimes they will have to rely upon their own resources entirely, lest they form the bad habit of always following up the efforts of others, and so fail to learn how to attempt and find out things for themselves. But when they see with sufficient understanding what ought to be said, the task of the teacher will be nearing completion: if they still make mistakes they will have to be brought back once more to their instructor.

7. We see birds doing the same kind of thing: they bring food in their beaks and share it amongst their young ones while they are still callow and weak; but when they appear full-grown, the parent birds fly before them and teach them to go out a little way from the nest and fly round their home; then, when their strength has been tested, they entrust them to the open sky and to their own self-reliance.

CHAPTER 7

LEARNING BY HEART

1. THERE is one common practice which I think should be radically altered in the case of pupils of the ages with which we are now dealing; they ought not to have to learn by heart all their own compositions and to recite them, as the custom is, upon an appointed day. The demand for this, to be sure, comes chiefly from the fathers of our pupils who have the idea that their children are really busied in their studies only if they are declaiming on every possible occasion, whereas progress depends upon steady application above all else.

2. I would certainly have boys practise composition and be constantly employed in that exercise, but I would still more earnestly urge upon them to learn by heart selected passages from speeches or narratives or writings of any kind that are deserving of such care.

3. The memory will be more strenuously exercised in grappling to itself the creations of others rather than our own, and those who have been trained in this harder type of labour will, without difficulty, memorize their own compositions which are already familiar and will also grow accustomed to the best; they will always have within themselves something to imitate, and quite unconsciously, in the end, will reproduce that style of oratory which they have stored deep in their minds.

4. They will be abundantly supplied with a sound vocabulary of the best words, with a correct method of arranging them, and with figures of speech not fashioned artificially for a particular occasion, but

springing up spontaneously from their store as from a treasure house. There is the additional advantage of being able to quote apt sayings from individual writers, a gift which adds zest to conversation and is invaluable in pleading cases. For more authority attaches to statements which have not been composed for the immediate purpose of the case in hand, and frequently they win greater praise than if they were the speaker's own.

5. On occasion, however, pupils should be permitted to declaim their own compositions, that they may enjoy the fruit of their toil from that general applause which is the supreme object of the orator's ambition. Yet this, too, should only occur when they have produced a piece of work of unusual polish and distinction, that they may thus be given the due reward for their studious application and may rejoice to have been adjudged worthy to declaim in public.

CHAPTER 8

SHOULD THE TRAINING OF EACH PUPIL FOLLOW HIS NATURAL BENT?

1. It is usually and rightly esteemed an excellent thing in a teacher that he should be careful to mark diversity of gifts in those whose education he has undertaken, and to know in what direction nature inclines each one most. For in this respect there is an unbelievable variety, and types of mind are no less numerous than types of body.

2. This can be gathered even from the orators themselves, who differ one from another in their styles of speech so completely that no two are alike, even though most of them have fashioned themselves on the model of those whom they admired.

3. Accordingly, most teachers have thought it expedient to train each pupil in such a way as to foster by sound instruction his peculiar gifts, and so to develop varied endowments most effectively in the direction of their natural bent. Thus, as an expert in wrestling, entering a gymnasium full of boys, tests them in all sorts of ways, both in body and in mind, and then decides for which type of contest each one is to be trained,

4. so it is thought right that the teacher of eloquence, after shrewdly observing which are the pupils whose natures take most delight in the closely knit polished style of speaking and which prefer the rapier stroke, the weighty manner, the sweet, the bitter, the shining, the sophisticated, should so adapt himself to individual cases

5. that each may be brought on in the style in which he excels. Nature, we are told, gains strength when assisted by careful training, whereas one who is drawn away from his natural bent cannot achieve success in studies for which he is less well fitted, and he also by neglect enfeebles those gifts for the exercise of which he seems to have been born.

6. Now this view seems to me to be only partially true (I take it that in following where reason leads us we are allowed freedom of judgement even against accepted beliefs); it is certainly of fundamental importance to distinguish the peculiar gifts of individual pupils.

7. In the task of training these no one will dissuade us from arranging a definite choice of studies. One pupil will be better fitted for the study of history, another will have a gift for poetry, another will find the study of law profitable, some perhaps should be sent to work in the fields. The teacher of rhetoric will separate these gifts just as the trainer we have spoken of will turn out a runner or a boxer or a wrestler or some other type of athlete for the sacred games

8. But the pupil who is destined for a career as a public speaker will have to work, not at some one part only, but at every part of his subject, even if some of them appear more difficult to master; for training would be quite superfluous if natural endowment were sufficient in itself.

9. Thus, to take examples, if a pupil comes into our hands who is by nature faulty in taste and turgid in style(as, indeed, most pupils are), shall we suffer him to go on in his own way? Where we find that which is dry and barren, shall we not nourish and, as it were,

clothe it? If it is necessary to remove certain defects, why should we not be permitted to add something?

10. Not that I am fighting against nature: I do not hold that any good gift of nature should be neglected, but I do maintain that such a gift should be fostered and that what is lacking should be supplied.

11. Let me recall to you the famous teacher Isocrates, whose writings testify to his genius as a speaker as eloquently as do his pupils to his excellence as a teacher. When he made his pronouncement upon Ephorus and Theopompus, saying that the one needed the bit and the other the spur, did he consider that the slowness in the one, who was more sluggish, or the impetuosity of the other's wellnigh breakneck speed should be encouraged by their teacher? Not at all; he thought that the natural gifts of the two should be blended.

12. Less gifted natures, to be sure, may so far receive indulgence as to be led only to the measure of achievement to which nature calls them. For thus they will do better all that they can manage. But if more generously endowed material is entrusted to us with which we may with justice have formed hopes of moulding a real orator, no kind of excellence in speaking is to be neglected.

13. For though such a nature may have a stronger bent in some one direction, as is inevitable, yet it will not be wholly set against all other branches of our studies, and with care it will bring them to the same level of perfection as those in which it excelled. Just so (to stick to our example) the expert in physical training will not, if he has undertaken to train a pancratiast, only teach him to strike with the fist or with the heel,

or wrestling-holds only, and of these a certain limited number, but everything that belongs to that sort of contest. There will be some one who will not manage them all: he will devote his energies to what he can accomplish.

14. For there are two things which must at all costs be avoided. The first is attempting the impossible, and the second transferring a pupil from what he does best to something else for which he is less fitted. But if our pupil is a Nicostratus—such as we saw when we were young and he was an old man—in his case the teacher will utilize every branch of training alike and make him invincible as Nicostratus was, both in wrestling and in boxing, in both of which contests he was crowned on the same occasion.

15. And how much more care will have to be taken by the instructor of the future orator! It is not enough to speak in subdued tones only or in close-knit level argument or with austere severity, any more than it is right for the speech-training expert to excel in rendering high notes only or medium or deep ones or even particular subdivisions of them. For like a harp, so a speech is not perfect unless, from the lowest to the highest note, it is in tune with all its strings at proper tension.

CHAPTER 9

THE DUTY OF THE PUPIL

1. HAVING dealt at length with the duties of teachers, I confine my advice to pupils to one precept in the meantime, to wit, that they should love their teachers no less than their studies themselves and should regard them as the parents not indeed of their bodies but of their minds.

2. Such dutiful affection will greatly aid their work. For thus they will listen with willing ear and believe what they are told, and strive to resemble their instructors; and again they will gather in their classrooms with joyful eagerness, will not resent correction, will rejoice in being praised, and by their zeal will strive to win their teacher's love.

3. For as it is the duty of the one to teach, so it is the duty of these others to prove themselves apt to learn: otherwise neither is sufficient without the other. And as the birth of man results from the union of his parents, and as you will scatter seed in vain unless the furrow softened to receive it gives it nourishment, so eloquence cannot grow to full maturity save by the harmonious co-operation of him who gives and him who receives instruction.

(*The remaining chapters of Book II are concerned with a general discussion of the nature and purpose of rhetoric, and are of less immediate interest to the student of education.*)

BOOK XII

INTRODUCTION

1. I HAVE now reached that part of my design which is by far the most important. Indeed, had I been able in sketching out the work even vaguely to appreciate its difficulty, as I do now in striving to carry it out, I should have bethought me long ago of the limitations of my powers. But at first the shame I would incur by the non-fulfilment of my promise kept me to the task: afterwards, though difficulties were increasing at almost every step, I forced myself to persevere through them all that I might not sacrifice what had already been accomplished.

2. And so now, too, though my burden is heavier than ever, yet with the end in view I am determined to faint rather than to give in. I did not realize the adventurous nature of the voyage upon which we embarked so modestly. Having launched forth, wooed by the breeze as it were, we sailed a little farther, still, however, engaged in the exposition of familiar topics such as have been dealt with by most writers of handbooks on rhetoric, not far from the shore as it seemed, and in company with many who had, so to speak, ventured to trust themselves to the same breezes.

3. Then, when we came to deal with the theory of style, a recent discovery which very few have attempted to deal with, scarce was a sail visible so far away from port. And now, when the orator we were engaged in training has left the teachers of rhetoric and is either being carried along by the force of his own eloquence or is seeking further aid from the inmost shrine of

wisdom (i.e. philosophy), we begin to realize how far we have been carried out on to the deep.

4. Now 'The sky is all about us and all about us is the sea', and in all that vast expanse we seem to descry but one other voyager, Marcus Tullius, and even he, though he has launched upon this sea in so large and so well-found a vessel, is lessening sail and checking his oarsmen and is satisfied to conclude with a discussion of the type of eloquence a finished orator will employ. But our reckless daring will even attempt to sketch the orator's character and assign him duties. Thus I cannot overtake my great predecessor and yet I must go farther than he, as my subject demands it. Yet zeal in so noble a cause deserves to win approval, and it betrays what may be called a safer kind of recklessness to essay a task wherein indulgence is more easily come by.

CHAPTER 1

THE ORATOR MUST BE A GOOD MAN

1. LET our ideal orator, then, conform to the definition of Marcus Cato, 'a good man, skilled in speaking'. In any case let him be what Cato put first and what is by nature the more important and the greater thing, viz. a good man. And that not only for this reason that if the power of speech were enlisted in the service of wickedness there would be nothing more harmful to public and private interests than eloquence, and we ourselves who have done our best to contribute something towards skill in speaking would have done mankind grievous disservice in fashioning these weapons not for a soldier but for a brigand.

2. Why do I speak of myself? Even Nature, in respect of that peculiar gift which as it appears she has bestowed on man, distinguishing him thereby from other animals, would prove to be no true parent but a step-mother, if she intended fluency of speech to be the accomplice of crime, the betrayer of innocence, the enemy of truth. For it were better that men be born dumb and lack all power of reasoning than that they should employ the gifts of Providence for mutual destruction.

3. Nay, my judgement in this matter goes farther. Not only do I assert that the orator ought to be a good man, I say that no one will be an orator unless he is a good man. Surely you cannot admit discernment in those, who, when faced with a choice between good and evil, prefer to follow the baser course, or foresight in men who through their own actions expose them-

selves, at an unexpected turn of events, to the gravest penalties not infrequently of the law and always of a guilty conscience.

4. And if it is not only a saying amongst wise men but also a matter of common belief that no one but a fool is wicked, surely the orator will never be a fool. A further point is this, that the mind cannot concentrate even upon the pursuit of the noblest ideal unless it be free from all vice: first, because the same breast cannot harbour both good and evil, and it is no more possible for the same mind to think the best and the worst thoughts at the same time than it is for a man to be at once good and bad.

5. In the next place for this reason also, that a mind which is absorbed in such an ideal must be free from all other interests, even those that are without blame. For thus, and thus only, free and entire, with nothing to hinder or distract it, it will fix its single gaze upon the object of its quest.

6. If too much care given to estates, over-anxious devotion to money-making, the pleasure of the chase, and days devoted to public spectacles all encroach seriously upon our studies (for time is lost to one thing that is given to another), what think you will be the effects of greed, avarice, and envy, whose lawless fancies disturb even men's slumbers and the dreams of sleep?

7. Nothing is so burdened, so changeable, so torn and distracted by countless varied passions as is the evil mind. When it is plotting guile it is harassed by hope, anxiety, and toil: when it has accomplished its evil purpose it is tormented by uneasiness, remorse, and dread of all manner of penalties. What room is there amid such distractions for letters or any noble

accomplishment? No more assuredly than there is for corn on ground cumbered with thorns and brambles.

8. Come, is not temperance essential if we are to endure the toil of study? What hope, then, is there in lust and luxury? Does not love of praise spur us on more than aught else in our literary pursuits? But do we think that bad men care for praise? Moreover, it is obvious that the major portion of a speech consists in discussing what is just and good. Will an evil and unjust man speak of these things in a way that befits their dignity?

9. Finally, to dismiss the greater part of this inquiry, let us grant what is really impossible, that the best man and the worst have the same natural ability, the same application, the same training—which will prove the better speaker? Surely he who is also the better man. The same man, then, will never be at once evil and a perfect orator. For nothing is perfect that is surpassed by something else.

10. Still, that we may not seem in Socratic fashion, to frame answers to suit ourselves, let it be granted that there is some one so blindly set against the truth as to venture to maintain that the bad man endowed with the same ability, application, and training as the good man will be just as good an orator as he. Let us prove the folly of this opponent, too.

11. Surely no one will doubt this, that the purpose of any speech is to make the case put forward seem true and righteous to the jury? Now which will succeed more easily in the task of persuasion, the good man or the bad? The good man, of course, will usually say what is true and righteous.

12. But even if on occasion at the call of duty

(a thing which may happen, as I shall show presently) he tries to present a false case, he will of necessity be listened to with greater confidence. In the case of bad men, owing to their contempt for what men think and their ignorance of what is right, even the pretence of truth and righteousness breaks down at times. And so they make unreasonable claims and shameless statements.

13. These are backed up with unseemly obstinacy and fruitless toil in the pursuit of ends which certainly cannot be achieved. For just as in their lives, so in their cases, their hopes are insatiate. It often happens that even when they speak the truth they are not believed, and to have a man of such character to plead a case condemns it right away.

14. Now I must meet the objections which I can see launched at me by wellnigh universal consent. Was Demosthenes, then, not an orator? Yet we have it on record that he was a bad man. Was Cicero no orator? Yet many have found fault with his moral character also. What am I to do? I must face the storm of indignation my answer will arouse, but I must first soothe the feelings of my audience.

15. It does not seem to me that Demosthenes is so deserving of bitter obloquy that I should credit all the charges heaped upon him by his enemies, when I read his splendid public utterances and the noble story of his death;

16. nor do I see that Marcus Tullius at any point in his career lacked the true spirit of a loyal citizen. The proof lies in his glorious achievements as consul, his blameless conduct as provincial governor, his refusal to act upon the board for the partition of Campania, his constancy during those calamitous civil wars

which fell within his lifetime, a constancy unmoved by hope or fear and never wavering in allegiance to the righteous cause of the republic.

17. Some think he lacked courage: to them he has himself made an excellent reply, that he was 'timid not in enduring dangers but in striving to avoid them'. And this he proved by the very manner of his death, which he met with unwavering fortitude.

18. But if these men did lack the highest virtue, to those who ask me if they were orators I shall reply in the manner of the Stoics when they are asked if Zeno was a wise man or Cleanthes or Chrysippus, 'these were indeed great men and worthy of all reverence, yet they did not reach the full perfection of man's nature'.

19. Even Pythagoras did not choose to be called wise like those who went before him, but rather a seeker after wisdom. Still following the ordinary practice in speaking, I have often said, and shall say again, that Cicero was a perfect orator, just as in ordinary speech we call our friends good and prudent, terms which properly apply only to the perfectly wise man. But when I have to speak exactly and in strict conformity with truth, I shall still be in search of that perfect orator whom Cicero himself was seeking.

20. I admit that he stands upon the very pinnacle of eloquence, and can scarcely imagine any possible addition that would improve his oratory, but rather might perchance discover passages which I may think he would ultimately have removed; that, indeed, is pretty much the verdict of expert critics, viz. that he had countless excellences and also some defects, and he himself bears witness that he pruned much of his youthful exuberance. Yet since he never claimed for

himself the name of wisdom, albeit fully conscious of his merits and, since he could have spoken better had longer life been granted him and a more tranquil age in which to compose his speeches, we should not do him an injustice in believing that he did not reach the very highest point, though no one has come nearer to it.

21. If I felt otherwise, I might defend this position with greater force and freedom. Or while Marcus Antonius asserted that he never saw an eloquent speaker (which is far less than the perfect orator) and even Marcus Tullius himself had not yet discovered him and only pictured and imagined him, can I dare to deny that in the vast eternity of time to come something may be found more perfect than aught that has been hitherto?

22. I pass by those who fail to do justice to Cicero and Demosthenes, even in the sphere of eloquence: yet Cicero himself does not think Demosthenes quite perfect, saying that he sometimes nods, nor does Cicero seem perfect either to Brutus and Calvus, who actually censure faults in his composition in letters addressed to Cicero himself, or to the two Asinii, who in several passages make quite bitter attacks upon his style.

23. Suppose we grant, though nature by no means allows it, that there has been found a bad man who is supremely eloquent: even so I will refuse him the name of orator, just as I cannot concede the name of brave man to all who have shown themselves prompt in action, for bravery has no meaning apart from virtue.

24. Does not he who is called in to plead cases require an integrity which no greed can corrupt, no influence seduce, no fear overawe? Shall we then bestow

the sacred name of orator upon a traitor, a renegade, a sham defender? Nay, if even advocates of moderate ability profit by possessing what is commonly styled goodness, why should not the perfect orator, who never has existed but yet may exist, be perfect, as well in moral character as in eloquence?

25. It is no mere forensic hack that we are training, no hireling voice, no plodding advocate, to call him by no harsher name, such as is commonly styled *causidicus* (pleader); no, it is a man endowed with genius, one whose training has embraced the whole circle of the liberal arts, a gift of heaven to earth such as no age has ever seen, peerless and perfect in every aspect, a man of noble thought and noble speech.

26. For such a man how small a field will there be in the protection of the innocent, the conviction of the wicked, or in the championing of truth against falsehood in trivial suits involving money? In such tasks, too, no doubt he will show himself supreme, but his genius will shine forth more brightly in greater ones, when a senate's policy has to be guided or a people's folly checked.

27. Was it not such a man that Virgil seems to have imagined, assigning him the task of soothing the populace when stones and fire-brands are already flying?

> If then some grave and pious man appear
> They hush their noise and lend a listening ear.

We have then before all else a good man; after this he will add 'skilled in speaking':

> He soothes with sober words their angry mood
> And quenches their innate desire for blood.
>
> (Dryden's *Virgil.*)

28. In war, too, will not this same man whom we are training, if the soldiers are to be heartened for the fray, in his address draw upon the inmost truths of philosophy? For how, when men are entering into battle, can all those fears of toil, of pain, of death itself, be banished from their minds unless they are replaced by love of country, courage, and the living image of the good?

29. And these he will best bring home who has first taught them to himself. Hypocrisy betrays itself no matter how it be concealed, nor can there be a fluency of utterance which will not halt and hesitate if word and thought chime not together. Now a bad man must say one thing and think another.

30. Good men will never be at a loss for noble speech and sterling subject-matter (for they will be wise as well), and even if their speech lacks showy trappings it is by its own nature sufficiently adorned and no righteous utterance is lacking in eloquence.

31. Wherefore let our youth, nay all of us of every age (for it is never too late for noble aspirations), strive with all our minds towards this goal and labour at this task; it may be our good fortune to succeed. For if nature does not forbid the existence of a good man, and of one skilled in speaking, why should not some one combine these in himself? And why should not each man hope that he will be the one to do so?

32. Even if our mental powers fall short of this, yet we shall be the better in both respects, in proportion to our progress. This idea at any rate we must banish from our minds, that eloquence, fairest of all things, can be combined with mental depravity. Fluency of speech in bad men must itself be reckoned bad; for it makes yet worse men of those who possess it.

33. Methinks I hear this argument advanced by certain critics (for there always will be men who prefer eloquence to goodness): Why then is there so much art in eloquence? Why have you discoursed upon rhetorical colouring, the pleading of difficult cases, and at some length even upon confession of guilt, if it is not the case that vigour and fluency of speech sometimes overthrow truth itself? A good man only pleads good causes and, even without the aid of learning, such causes are safeguarded by their intrinsic truth.

34. In reply to these critics I shall defend my own book, and then I shall satisfy them as regards the duty of a good man when he feels called upon to defend the guilty. It is useful to discuss methods of speaking on the side of untruth or even, on occasion, of injustice, if only for this reason, that it makes it easier to detect and to refute them; just as a doctor will make better use of remedies if he knows what drugs are harmful.

35. The philosophers of the Academy, after arguing both for and against virtue, will not choose the vicious way of life, nor was the great Carneades himself an unjust man though it is said that at Rome, in the hearing of Cato the Censor, he argued against justice with as much vehemence as he had employed upon the previous day in its defence. Nay, the real nature of virtue is revealed by vice, its opposite; justice is more clearly understood by a consideration of injustice and many things are proved by their contraries. An orator, then, should know his adversary's plans just as a general should know those of his enemy.

36. Good reasons can be adduced even in support of a course which when first stated seems difficult to defend, viz. that a good man in pleading should on

occasion desire to withhold the truth from the jury. If any one is surprised that I should put this forward (though it is not simply my own view but that of men acknowledged in antiquity to have been the greatest masters of wisdom), let him reflect that many things are good or evil not so much in their results as in their causes.

37. It is often good to slay a man, sometimes it is most noble to put one's own children to death; and, when the common weal demands it, it is permitted to do things yet more terrible to speak of. We cannot, therefore, regard merely the nature of the case a good man is pleading but also his purpose and motive.

38. And first all must grant me what is admitted even by the most rabid of the Stoics, that a good man will on occasion tell a lie, sometimes indeed in matters of but slight importance: just as when dealing with children who are ill we pretend many things for their welfare's sake and make many promises which we do not intend to fulfil.

39. Much less are we bound to tell the truth when an assassin is to be prevented from murdering some one, or an enemy deceived for our country's sake, so that what at one time is blameworthy, even in a slave, may at another time be praiseworthy in the wise man himself; if this be established, I see many possible reasons which justify a good man in undertaking such cases as he would have refused in the absence of an honourable motive.

40. I do not mean pleading for a father, a brother, or a friend in time of danger, for I believe we ought to submit to the law in such cases, even if it be too severe: yet there is ample ground for hesitation when the

images of justice and affection are ranged against each other. Let us remove all doubt. Supposing some one has plotted against a tyrant and is on his trial for so doing, will the orator as we have defined him not desire his acquittal, or if he undertakes the case will he not defend him by misrepresentation, just as much as one who is arguing a bad case?

41. Or supposing a judge is going to condemn certain noble actions unless we prove that they were not done? Will not the orator employ even these questionable methods to save one who is not merely innocent but also worthy of praise for his loyalty? What if we know of certain things which are naturally just but at a certain juncture inexpedient for the State, shall we not, to prevent them, use an art of speech which is indeed good but which so far resembles what is evil?

42. Moreover, no one will doubt that, if the guilty can somehow be changed into good citizens (as is admitted sometimes to be possible), it is more advantageous to the state that they should be saved than that they should be punished. If it be clear, then, to the orator that the prisoner who is really guilty will be a good man, will he not try to save him?

43. Imagine now that a charge clearly true is brought against an able general without whom the country cannot overcome the enemy: will not the common weal summon the orator to his defence? There is the famous case of Fabricius and Cornelius Rufinus. Though the latter was in general a bad citizen and a personal enemy of his, Fabricius, because he knew him to be a good leader on an occasion when war threatened, openly gave his vote to make him consul and said to certain people who wondered why he did it

that he preferred to be robbed by a fellow citizen rather than sold by the enemy. And so, had he been an orator, would he not also have defended Rufinus even if he were undoubtedly guilty of embezzlement?

44. Many such cases might be mentioned: it is enough to quote a single one. For we are not concerned to argue that our ideal orator should often take up such cases: but that, if such considerations compel him to do so, the definition still remains true, viz. that the orator is a good man skilled in speaking.

45. It is likewise necessary to teach and to learn the methods of handling difficult cases. For often even the best cases resemble bad ones and an innocent man is entangled in the meshes of circumstantial evidence: so that he must be defended by the same method of argument which would be employed if he were guilty. Good causes and bad ones have very many things in common—witnesses, documents, suspicions, prejudices: and probability is established or disproved in the same way as the truth. And so the speech will be adapted to the circumstances but the motive behind it will always be an honourable one.

CHAPTER 2

THE ORATOR MUST KNOW HOW CHARACTER IS FORMED

1. THE orator, then, is a good man and such a man cannot be conceived without moral excellence; moral excellence, though it derives certain impulses from nature, must yet be perfected by training. Before all else the orator must in his studies cultivate morality, and he must deal with all subjects that touch upon the honourable and the just, for without these no one can be either a good man or skilled in speaking.

2. Unless perchance we agree with those who think that morals come by nature and are in no way helped by training; as though forsooth the very meanest handicraft admittedly requires a teacher, but virtue, the gift whereby man might approach most nearly to the gods, has come to us unsought and without effort simply because we have been born. Will that man be temperate who does not know what temperance is?

3. Or that man brave who has not by earnest thought driven from him the fear of pain, of death, of punishment hereafter? Or that man just who has not examined justice and goodness and never studied in some learned work the laws common by nature to all men and also those set up amid individual people and nations? How trifling must they consider that which they regard as so easy!

4. But I leave this point, which no one with the slightest tinge of culture will, I think, dispute. I pass on to the next consideration, which is that no one will be skilled enough even in speaking who has not plumbed

the depths of man's nature and formed his own moral character by study and reflection.

5. Lucius Crassus is right in saying, in the third book of Cicero's *De Oratore*, that everything that is said about equity, justice, truth, goodness, and their opposites, belongs to the orator's province, and that philosophers when they champion these with the force of eloquence are using the weapons of rhetoric, not their own. Yet he also admits that these must now be sought from philosophy, apparently because he thinks that philosophy is more fully in possession of them.

6. Hence, also, follows what Cicero maintains in several of his books and letters, viz. that fluency in speaking is derived from the deepest springs of wisdom and that accordingly the same men were for a time the teachers of morality and of eloquence.

Now this plea of mine does not mean that I desire the orator to be a philosopher, for no other group of men have withdrawn themselves more completely from the duties of citizenship and all the responsibilities of the orator.

7. What philosopher has ever attended the law courts with assiduity or won fame in popular assemblies? Which of them has taken part in the administration of the state, the main subject of the teaching of most of them? Nay, I would have my pupil a wise man of the Roman type showing himself truly a useful citizen, not by disputation behind closed doors but by practical experience and exertion.

8. But the study of philosophy, abandoned by those who have betaken themselves to eloquence, no longer occupies its proper sphere, here in the open spaces of

the forum, but has withdrawn first into the porticoes and wrestling schools and then into the lecture theatres. So that what the orator must have, and cannot get from the teachers of eloquence, he must of course seek from those with whom it has remained, by careful study of the authors who give instruction concerning virtue; and thus the life of the orator may be linked with a knowledge of things both human and divine.

9. How much greater and more beautiful would these things appear if the teachers of them could also discourse upon them with surpassing eloquence! Would that the day might come when some such perfect orator as we desire would win back this art which is now hated because of the insolent presumption and vice of those who corrupt its excellences and, as it were, reconquer it and restore it to the domain of eloquence.

10. Philosophy is divided into three parts, viz. natural philosophy, ethics, and dialectic (logic), and by which of these is it not associated with the work of the orator?

Taking them in the reverse order there can be no question about the last (dialectic) which is wholly concerned with words, seeing that it is the business of orators to know the exact meaning of each term, to clear up ambiguities, to disentangle confused statements, to judge of truth and falsehood, to prove or to refute what you will.

11. Dialectic, however, is not to be employed with the same subtlety and precision in pleading as in philosophical disputation, because the orator is bound not only to convince his hearers but also to move and to delight them, and for this he has need of a certain

degree of energy and strength and charm of manner; even as the current is stronger in rivers that flow between high banks with a great whirling flood than in shallow streams which even pebbles can obstruct.

12. Just as teachers of wrestling do not instruct their pupils in the various throws, as they call them, with the idea that those who have learned them should employ them all in the actual wrestling contest (for more depends on weight and steadiness and wind), but in order that they may have a reserve upon which to draw for one throw or the other, as opportunity offers;

13. So with this part of philosophy, dialectic, or if we prefer to call it so, the art of disputation: it is often useful in making limitations, inclusions, and distinctions, and in the solving of ambiguities by differentiation and division, as well as in leading an adversary on and getting him into difficulties. At the same time, if it takes entire control of a contest in the forum it will hinder the effectiveness of better methods and, by its very subtlety, will throw away the strength of the case in splitting it up to its own minuteness.

14. Thus you will find some who are wonderfully skilful in disputation, but who, when they cease hair-splitting, are not equal to the weight of a serious piece of pleading, like certain small animals which are swift in movement in a confined space but are easy to catch in the open.

15. Next, the moral part of philosophy, which is called ethics, of a surety is entirely within the orator's province. Amid the endless variety of cases, as we have shown in earlier books, in which some points are sought out by conjecture, others are settled by definition, others are barred by law or removed to another

court, others are proved by deductive reasoning or collide with each other or are split up because of legal ambiguity, in all of them hardly one can be mentioned which does not involve some discussion of equity and goodness, whilst we are all aware that very many turn entirely upon some question of morality.

16. In deliberative oratory again, what method of exhortation is there apart from the question of honour? And what of the third division of oratory, which includes the duty of assigning praise and blame? Surely it is concerned with the discussion of right and wrong.

17. Will the orator not dilate upon justice, courage, temperance, self-control, and dutiful affection? Our ideally good man, who not merely knows these virtues as words and names, and has not merely heard them to repeat them with his lips, but who has taken them to his bosom and thinks in accordance with them, will have no difficulty in pondering them and will speak truly that which he knows.

18. Since every general question is wider in range than any question concerning particulars, because the part is contained in the whole and the universal is not added to the particular, assuredly no one will doubt that general questions are especially associated with philosophical studies.

19. Now there are many points which require to be made clear by brief and appropriate definitions (hence the class of cases where the question at issue is spoken of as one of definition); must not the orator be equipped for this task, too, by those who have made a special study of it? Nay, does not every question of equity turn either on the exact use of words, or the discussion of what justice is, or the discovery of a motive? And of

these some fall within the province of logic and some of ethics.

20. Oratory, then, if it be truly oratory, is by its nature intermingled with all these questions of philosophy, whilst mere fluency that lacks this training must go astray, having either no guides or guides that are deceitful.

Natural philosophy offers wider scope than any other branch for the practice of eloquence because one must speak of things divine in a loftier strain than of things human; it also embraces the whole department of ethics, without which, as we have shown, oratory is impossible.

21. If the universe is controlled by divine guidance, surely the state will have to be managed by good men. If our minds are of divine origin, surely we are bound to cling to virtue and not be slaves to the pleasures of an earthly body. Will the orator not touch constantly upon these themes? Will he not be bound to speak at length concerning omens and oracles and in fact everything of a religious nature, such questions being frequently the subjects of the senator's most serious debates—I mean if he is going to be as we wish him, a true citizen as well as an orator? How can we even imagine eloquence in a man who is ignorant of the highest of things?

22. If common sense did not support my views, yet surely we should be convinced by examples. Take the case of Pericles. His eloquence, though no specimens of it have survived, is said to have been characterized by a power almost too great to be believed. Such is the testimony of the historians and of the old writers of comedy, the most free-spoken of men. And he is

recorded to have been a pupil of Anaxagoras the natural philosopher. Similarly Demosthenes, greatest of all the Greek orators, is said to have studied under Plato.

23. Marcus Tullius of course often tells us that he owed more to the walks of the Academy than to the lecture-rooms of the teachers of rhetoric. Nor would his eloquence have gushed forth in so mighty a stream had he limited his genius to the forum and not let it range freely to the farthest bounds of the universe.

There now arises a further question: which school of philosophers is most useful for eloquence? There are not many which can contest the palm in this respect.

24. First Epicurus puts himself out of the running, for he bids his followers fly from all scientific training as fast as ever they can go. Aristippus, who places the supreme good in bodily pleasures, does not urge us to endure such toil. What share can Pyrrhon have in our pursuits? He cannot be sure of the existence of the jury he is to address, of the prisoner whom he is to defend, of the senate before whom he is to state his views.

25. Some regard the Academy as most useful because the practice of arguing on both sides of a question resembles most nearly the preliminary exercises for pleading in the forum. As a proof they add the fact that this school has produced very eminent orators. The Peripatetics also boast of their achievements in the field of oratory. They practically invented the exercise of speaking on general questions for the sake of practice.

The Stoics, whilst they must admit that their teachers have lacked richness and splendour in eloquence, maintain none the less that they are unexcelled in strictness of demonstration and subtlety of reasoning.

26. Such are the rival claims of the philosophers. As though bound by an oath or forbidden by some religious scruple, they think it a sin to depart from the tenets they have once embraced. But an orator has no need to swear allegiance to any sect.

27. For his is a greater and a nobler task, I mean that for which he is a candidate, if he is going to win praises for the perfection both of his life and of his eloquence. Accordingly he will set before himself as models all the most eloquent speakers and for the moulding of his character he will pick out the noblest precepts and follow the straight path towards virtue. He will use every kind of training, but will devote himself most to the highest and the noblest.

28. What richer topic for a weighty and eloquent speech can be found than virtue, the state, providence, the origin of mind, friendship? These are subjects to which mind and speech rise together, viz. what is truly good, what soothes fear, checks evil desires, raises us above common prejudice, and proves our minds divine.

29. Not only the dictates of philosophy, but still more the noble deeds of history, must be known and pondered well. And assuredly nowhere will you find a richer store than in the records of the Roman people.

30. Will the lessons of courage, justice, honour, self-control, simplicity, contempt for pain and death, be taught by any better than by such heroes as Fabricius, Curius, Regulus, Decius, Mucius, and countless others? As the Greeks excel in precepts, so the Romans excel in examples, which is better far.

31. Nor will our orator rest content with a knowledge of these only (without imitating them), for he

will not be satisfied to regard the immediate present and to-day alone, but will consider the whole range of men's remembrance in the days to come as the field for an honourable life and the arena in which fame is to be won. And from such sources let him drink deep draughts of justice, let him win courage and sincerity to adorn his pleadings in the forum and his speeches in the Senate. For he will not be a perfect orator unless he has the knowledge and the courage to speak out honestly what he believes.

[*The chapters which follow (XII. 3 to XII. 9) deal with such technical matters as these: the importance to an orator of a knowledge of law and history, the adjuncts of oratory (self-confidence, physical strength, grace of movements, &c.), the proper age at which to begin pleading, points to be noted in preparing and in arguing cases.*

Chapter 10 of Book XII is entitled 'Styles in Oratory' and opens with a discussion of the various schools. The respective merits of Attic and Asiatic oratory are canvassed and the natural limitations of Roman eloquence indicated. We resume at 40.]

CHAPTER 10

STYLE IN ORATORY

40. SOME think there is no natural eloquence save that which most closely resembles the everyday speech in which we converse with friends, wives, children, or slaves and which is content to express our meaning without anything of a studied or elaborate kind. They hold that to go beyond this in speaking is affectation and vainglorious show, departure from truth, a mere

juggling with words, whose sole function, assigned to them by nature, is to give expression to our meaning.

41. In the same way, they point out, the bodies of athletes, though they become stronger through exercise and dieting, are not in a natural condition and do not conform to man's normal appearance. What is the good, they ask, of discussing things in a roundabout way and in metaphors, that is in words that are either superfluous or inappropriate, seeing that every single thing has its own appropriate designation?

42. Finally, they maintain that the earliest orators employed the most natural style; that they were followed by others more nearly resembling the poets, and holding like them, though in a less pronounced fashion, that there is merit in what is false and inappropriate. There is some truth in their contention, and we should not depart as far as some do from apt and simple language.

43. Yet, as I said in dealing with composition, if a speaker has added some eloquence to a perfectly bald statement (all that is strictly necessary), he is not to be blamed on this count. For it seems to me that there is an essential difference between ordinary conversation and the speech of an eloquent man. If it were enough for an orator merely to convey his meaning, he would take no special pains beyond selecting appropriate words; but since he has to please, to move, to stir the mind of his hearer to countless emotions, he will employ those aids which nature herself has given to man.

44. It is natural to harden our muscles by exercise, to increase our strength, to improve our colour. In every land one man is accounted more eloquent than another and sweeter-tongued; if it were not so all

would be equal and the same style would suit every man; but in their speech men preserve their individuality. Thus the more effective a man's oratory the nearer does he approach the real nature of eloquence.

45. I am not, then, inclined to quarrel with those who think that we must concede something to a modern audience that demands what is sparkling and clear; and I do not think the orator should swear allegiance to the style of those who spoke before Cato and the Gracchi, or even to those speakers themselves. I note that it was the practice of Marcus Tullius, whilst directing all his efforts to the winning of the case, to take some thought also for the pleasure of his hearers; thus he held he was benefiting himself and his client as well. For he benefited him just in proportion to the pleasure he gave.

46. I cannot imagine how we could add to the pleasure given by his speeches, unless, indeed, by more epigrams. That, of course, is possible without detriment to the treatment of his themes and the authority of his utterance, provided that those flashes are not too numerous and close together and that they do not interfere with each other.

47. But while I concede so much, let no one press me further. To modern taste I allow that the gown should not be of rough wool, but not that it should be of silk; that the head should be shorn, but not adorned with waves and ringlets, and I admit that, short of luxury and extravagance, elegance and seemliness are one.

48. As regards what we commonly call epigrams (the ancients and the Greeks, in particular, did not employ them, but I find a few specimens in Cicero), who would deny their usefulness, provided they are relevant, not too numerous, and likely to help the case?

They catch the attention of your hearers, often decide the issue by a single stroke, and by reason of their very brevity are better remembered and, whilst they please, persuade.

49. Some consider that these brilliant flashes, while permissible in speech, should be excluded from written speeches. I must not, therefore, omit to deal with this point, viz. that many men of learning have drawn a distinction between the methods of speaking and of writing. As they point out, many most famous orators have left to posterity nothing destined to live in literature—Pericles, for instance, and Demades—while others again, who were excellent at composing speeches, were not equal to the task of delivering them—such was Isocrates.

50. They argue further that, in pleading, vigour is more effective and pleasing effects are sought somewhat more freely, for the minds of an unlettered audience have to be moved and guided; but what is committed to books and put forth as a model must be correct and polished and composed in accordance with law and rule, because it comes into the hands of learned men and has skilled craftsmen to criticize it as a work of art.

51. Nay, these clever teachers (for they have persuaded themselves and many another that such they are) hold that the method of induction is better suited for speaking and that of syllogism for writing. My own view is that good speaking and good writing are one and the same, and that a written speech is simply a record of the conduct of a case. It ought, therefore, to possess every kind of excellence; every excellence I say, not every defect. For I am aware that what is defective

is sometimes pleasing to the unlettered. How then will writing and speaking differ?

52. Were you to give me a select audience of wise critics, I should cut out a great deal from the speeches not only of Cicero but even of Demosthenes, who is far more restrained. In such hearers no emotions are to be excited, nor are their ears to be soothed by words of pleasant sound; with them, so Aristotle thinks, no preliminaries are required, for wise men will not be influenced by them; it is enough to set forth the subject in pointed and appropriate language and to marshal the evidence that proves your case.

53. But when we have to plead before the populace, or some of their number, and those who are going to pass sentence are, as not infrequently happens, uneducated men or even yokels, we must employ every device which we believe will serve to drive home the point we are striving to make. These devices will appear in our speeches and should be indicated when we write, if our purpose in writing is to show how one ought to speak.

54. Would Demosthenes have done badly in pleading as he wrote, or Cicero? Do we recognize them as matchless pleaders otherwise than by their writings? Was their pleading better or worse than their writing? If it was worse, they should have spoken as they wrote; if it was better, they should have written as they spoke.

55. Will the orator, then, always plead as he writes? Always, if it be possible. But if the time assigned by the court be too short, much that could be said will be cut out; all this will appear in the written version. And certain passages adapted to the capacity of the jury will not be written down as they were spoken, lest they be

attributed to the design of the orator and not to the peculiar circumstances of the case.

56. It is, indeed, most important to know how the jury will take what you have to say and, as Cicero teaches us, the face of the juryman is the speaker's guide. You must therefore emphasize what you know is pleasing to the jury and avoid what will not be acceptable. You must even choose the way of speaking which may most easily appeal to them. And that is not surprising when we consider that changes are often made to suit the peculiarities of witnesses.

57. For instance, he was a wise counsel who after asking a clown of a witness whether he knew Amphion and being answered in the negative, dropped the rough breathing and shortened the second syllable of the name, whereupon the witness knew him very well indeed in that form. Thus it sometimes happens that the spoken and the written versions differ, as we are not always allowed to speak as we ought to write.

[*In sections* 58–68 *Quintilian deals with the accepted division of oratory into three styles: the plain style, the grand style, and an intermediate type to which the name 'florid' or 'flowery'* (*Greek* ἀνθηρός) *is applied. Having illustrated these and made it clear that the division is not an exhaustive one, he proceeds.*]

69. There are, then, many types of eloquence and it is foolish to ask which one an orator is to adopt; for every style, provided it is sound, has its appropriate use and the whole question of what is commonly called style in oratory is within the orator's discretion.

He will use all styles, as occasion demands, not merely in different cases but even in different parts of the same case.

70. He will not speak in the same manner in a case involving capital punishment as he will in a case of a disputed inheritance or on subjects like injunctions, guarantees, or money on loan; he will observe the distinctions between utterances in the Senate, at public meetings, and in private deliberations, and he will make constant variations to suit differences of persons, places, and times; thus in the same speech he will use different methods to rouse the jury and to placate them; he will not seek to draw anger and pity from the same sources, he will employ different arts in conveying information and in moving the emotions.

71. He will not limit himself to a uniform tone in introduction, exposition, proof, digression, or conclusion. He will speak weightily, austerely, fiercely, with spirit, with animation, with fluency, bitterly, in friendly wise, carelessly, carefully, smoothly, gently, sweetly, with brevity, with wit: not always the same, yet never inconsistent with himself.

72. Thus will be realized the most important function of oratory, viz. that the orator should speak effectively and with ability to secure his aim, and at the same time he will win the applause not only of learned critics but also of ordinary men.

73. It is an entire fallacy to suppose that more popularity and a greater meed of applause are to be won by a faulty and corrupt style of speaking which either vaunts itself in verbal licence or wantons in childish epigrams or is swollen with bombast or revels in empty platitudes or is decked with posies that will fall at the lightest touch or mistakes extravagance for sublimity or seeks to grace the ravings of a madman with the name of free speech.

74. That such a style does please many I do not deny, nor am I surprised at the fact. For eloquence of any sort is pleasing to the ear and will win applause, and every utterance of the human voice lures men's minds by a natural attraction; hence the knots of listeners in our public squares and by the Embankment. It is not then surprising that every pleader has his ring of loafers ready to listen to him.

75. When anything out of the ordinary in the way of eloquence falls upon the ears of the unlettered mob, no matter what it be, provided they have no hope of equalling it themselves, it wins their admiration, and rightly enough; for even to rise above the rank and file is not an easy thing. But such achievements vanish and fade away in comparison with nobler flights of eloquence, 'just as wool dyed red pleases us when we have no purple; but when you compare it with a cloak of Tyrian hue, it is outclassed by the appearance of the better dye', to borrow the words of Ovid.

76. And if you should apply a keener criticism to these faulty efforts, as you would sulphur to dyed fabrics, they would lose the false colour by which they had deceived their audience and reveal a ghastly pallor which can hardly be described. Such utterances then shed light only in the absence of the sun, as certain small animals are phosphorescent in the dark. Finally, many approve what is bad, but none finds fault with what is good.

77. All the excellences of which I have spoken will be achieved by the orator not only in the highest degree but also with the greatest ease. For supreme power in speaking, such as is worthy of our admiration, is not achieved by anxious care, painful to the last degree,

that wears the speaker to a shadow and irks him constantly as with feverish zeal he alters words and wastes away in the task of weighing them and putting them together.

78. The perfect orator, shining, lofty, richly endowed, is master of all the stores of eloquence that surround him in their generous abundance. He who has reached the summit toils no more in the ascent. In climbing, the lowest levels are most toilsome; as you make progress, the slope is gentler and the soil more fertile.

79. And if with unflagging efforts you surmount these gentler slopes as well, you come to fruits not bought by toil, and flowers of every hue spring up unsought, but withering if they be not plucked from day to day. Not that fluency has not its limits without which it is neither praiseworthy nor healthful; the shining splendour too of which we have spoken needs manly discipline, and powers of invention must be controlled by judgement.

80. Thus will be achieved greatness without excess, sublimity without violence, courage without recklessness, austerity without mournfulness, weight without sloth, exuberance without wantonness, pleasantness without licence, solemnity without bombast. The same principle will apply to other qualities and, in general, safety will lie in the middle course, because extremes on either side are faults.

CHAPTER 11

CONCLUSION

1–5. (The orator must retire from practice before his powers begin to fail; he may well devote the closing years of his life to teaching.)

6. No one would wish that an art in which he himself excelled should cease to flourish and, besides, what is more honourable than to teach that which you know thoroughly well? Thus Cicero tells us Caelius was brought to him by his father; thus, as a master should, he trained Pansa, Hirtius, and Dolabella, declaiming for them and listening to their speeches daily.

7. In fact, I think we ought to consider it the happiest time of the orator's life when in retirement and devoted to study, free from all jealousy and far from strife, he has established his reputation and enjoys while still alive that reverence which is more often accorded after a man is dead, and sees what place he is to hold in the estimation of posterity.

8. For myself, I know that, as far as my modest abilities have permitted, I have presented plainly and simply, for the instruction of any who wished to learn, such lessons as I have gained from my own experience and all else that I have been able to find out for the purpose of the present work. And it is enough for a good man to have taught what he knows.

9. But I am afraid I may seem to be asking too much in requiring the same person to be at once a good man and skilled in speaking, or to be including too wide a range of learning in adding to all the subjects to be learned in youth a knowledge of ethics and of civil law

as well as of the traditional theory of rhetoric; and I fear that even those who believe that all these things are necessary for our purpose may shrink from the weary length of the task and abandon it in premature despair.

10. But, first of all, let them remind themselves of the mighty power of the human intellect and of its capacity to accomplish its designs; for men have been able by arts less important than oratory, though more difficult of attainment, to cross seas, to note the courses and the numbers of the stars, yea wellnigh to measure the universe itself. Then let them think how noble is our aim and how we should not shrink from any toil with such a prize in view.

11. Having grasped these points they will more easily come to realize that the road itself is not impassable or even difficult to traverse. For the prior and more important thing, viz. that we be good men, depends chiefly on the will; and if a man truly and honourably wills to be good, he can easily acquire the arts that teach virtue.

12. The tasks set before us are neither so involved nor so numerous that they cannot be mastered by the serious application of a few years only. It is disinclination that makes the work seem long; to train ourselves for an honourable and happy life is a brief task, if we enter upon it with confidence. Nature has created us to excel in mind, and to attain to higher things is so easy for those who wish it that to the true observer it is more a matter of surprise that bad men are so numerous.

13. As water is the proper element for fish, dry land for animals, and the air that surrounds us for birds, so surely it ought to be easier for man to live in accordance

with nature than at variance with it. For the rest, even if we measure our age not by the long stretch of age but by the brief flower of youth, there are years in abundance for all these studies. Orderly arrangement and methodical habits will shorten all our tasks.

14. The fault lies first with our instructors, who are anxious to retain the pupils they have got, partly through their desire to secure for a little longer time their petty fees, partly from vanity, to enhance the difficulty of the subject they profess, partly also from ignorance of teaching methods or carelessness.

And next the fault lies with ourselves who think it better to linger over what we have learned already than to learn what we do not yet know.

15. To speak of our own studies in particular, what is the use of declaiming in the schools for all the years so many men devote to it (to say nothing of those who spend almost their whole lives so) and to waste such pains upon imaginary cases when it is enough to devote a limited time to learning the nature of real pleading and the laws of eloquence?

16. I do not mean that practice in speaking should ever be dropped but simply that we should not grow old in the practice of a single kind. We could, whilst still at school, recognize and learn the precepts of right living and gain practice in the forum.

The principles of knowledge are such that they do not demand many years for their acquisition. It is a common thing for any one of the arts I have mentioned to be comprised in a few volumes, so little need is there of infinite space and endless teaching.

There remains experience, which quickly builds up strength and preserves what it has so built up.

17. Knowledge, too, grows daily, and yet in this connexion countless books must be read wherein are sought precedents in history and models in oratory. Amongst other things, we should seek to read the opinions of philosophers and lawyers, yet we need not read everything—though that is possible. But we ourselves make our time short.

18. How little time do we assign to study! Hours are wasted in the useless toil of social duty or in idling at the play or in the circus or at banquets. Add games of every sort and the mania for exercise; take away the time claimed by travel, holidays in the country, worry about finance, endless interruptions of a vicious sort, winebibbing and all manner of evil devices. And even such time as remains does not find us in a fit state for studious application.

19. But if all these hours were devoted to our studies, our life would seem long enough and its years amply sufficient for the task of learning, if we count only the hours of daylight, without the help of nights, of which a fair portion is more than enough for the sleep that any man requires. As it is, we count years of life, not of study.

20. Nor, indeed, if geometers and grammarians and professors of the other arts have devoted the whole of a long life to a single subject, does it follow that we should require several lives for several studies. For they were not learning their subjects right on till they were old men, but they were content to learn one subject only, and all those years were spent in practising rather than in acquiring their art.

21. To say nothing of Homer, in whom we find perfect mastery of every art or at least clear evidence

of such mastery, to pass over Hippias of Elis who not only boasted a knowledge of the liberal arts, but also wore garments, a ring, and shoes made by his own hands and aimed at being independent of any other man's work, we believe, with all the Greeks, that Gorgias made light of all the many handicaps of age and bade his hearers ask questions on any subject they liked to choose.

22. What art that is worthy of a man of letters is not to be found in Plato? How many lives did Aristotle devote to learning so as to include within his range of knowledge not only all that had to do with philosophers and orators but also the whole natural history of animals and plants? These great men had to discover sciences, we only have to learn them. Antiquity has furnished us with so many teachers, so many models, that no age can appear more happy in the accident of birth than ours, for whose instruction all past ages have conspired to labour.

23. And now, to take Roman instances, Marcus Cato, a great general, philosopher, orator, historian, learned alike in law and agriculture, amid all his labours in the field and his great contests in the forum, in an age devoid of culture, learned Greek when he was already stricken in years to prove to mankind that even old men can acquire such learning as they have set their hearts upon.

24. How many subjects—almost all—were taught by Varro! What adjunct to oratory was not possessed by Marcus Tullius? Why multiply examples? Even Cornelius Celsus, a man of modest talents, not only wrote on all subjects of a literary kind but also left us precepts on strategy, on husbandry, on medicine, and

by the very breadth of his design proved himself worthy to be credited with a knowledge of all these subjects.

25. But, I shall be told, it is hard to accomplish so great a task, and no one has been completely successful in doing so. First and foremost, it is enough to encourage us in our studies that success is within the nature of things and that what has not yet been done is still possible; and, further, that all great and admirable performances have had a time when they were first achieved.

26. Poetry, for instance, reached its supreme height in Homer and Virgil, eloquence in Demosthenes and Cicero. In short, everything that is best in its own sphere had not existed before. But even if one despairs of reaching the highest (though why should he do so if he lack not ability, health, opportunity, and instructors?), yet it is, as Cicero says, a fine achievement to take second or third place.

27. Even if a man cannot win the fame of an Achilles in war, he will not despise the reputation of an Ajax or a Diomede, and if he cannot be a Homer he will not scorn the glory of Tyrtaeus. Nay more, if men had always thought that no one would surpass the best that had been, those who are now the best would not have been so, nor after Lucretius and Macer would there have been a Virgil, nor after Crassus and Hortensius a Cicero, nor after them those who have since surpassed them.

28. Even granting that we cannot hope to outstrip them, yet there is great honour in treading in the footsteps of the great. Did Pollio and Messala, who began their pleading when Cicero held the citadel of eloquence, achieve but scanty honour in their lives and meagre

glory in the eyes of later generations? Besides, the development to the highest degree of the arts would be but a sorry service to humanity, if at a given time the best had been accomplished.

29. There is this further fact that even a moderate degree of eloquence brings with it substantial benefits and, if one estimates such studies merely by their usefulness, it is almost on a level with the perfection of the art. It would not be difficult to prove by examples whether old or new, that from no other source have men won more wealth and honour, closer friendships, greater present and future glory; but it would be unworthy of the craft of letters to exact this lesser gain from the noblest of all professions, whose practice, nay whose very acquirement, brings the richest rewards to our studies; to do so would be to act like those who say they seek not the virtues themselves, but the pleasure which is derived from them.

30. Let us, then, with all our hearts pursue the majesty of eloquence itself, the noblest gift of the immortal gods to man, without which all our deeds are mute and lack the light of present fame and remembrance by posterity; and let us ever strive towards the best, for in so doing we shall either reach the highest or at any rate see many below us.

31. Such are the observations, Victorius Marcellus, whereby it seems to me that I can further to the best of my ability the teaching of oratory; and if they be well conned they will bring to studious youth no great material advantage, it may be, but at any rate something which I desire more earnestly, the will to strive towards the good.

INDEX